ELIZABETH BARRETT BROWNING
THE HOPE END YEARS

The Border Lines Series

Series Editor: John Powell Ward

ELIZABETH BARRETT BROWNING
THE HOPE END YEARS

Barbara Dennis

Border Lines Series Editor
John Powell Ward

seren

seren is the book imprint of
Poetry Wales Press Ltd
Wyndham Street, Bridgend,
Mid Glamorgan, CF31 1EF
Wales

A CIP record for this book is available at the
British Library Cataloguing in Publication Data Office

ISBN 1-85411-099-3
1-85411-091-8 paperback

*The publisher acknowledges the financial support of the
Arts Council of Wales*

Cover illustration: Elizabeth aged 14,
portrait by Eliza Cliffe

Printed in Palatino by WBC Book Manufacturers, Bridgend

Contents

Abbreviations

For Paul and Robert

Preface: Hope End

On 24 August 1832 two carriages rumbled down the cobbled drive at Hope End which curved between the lawns from the tall domed house, past the rush fringed pools, and wound through the parkland pastures heavy with summer. Did the cattle look up curiously from their stands in the shade of the huge beech and chestnut trees, flicking away the flies as the carriages passed, their gaze following the two dwindling shapes through the gates by the little low lodge, finally disappearing into the dusty lane which led to Ledbury and Gloucester, Bath and eventually Sidmouth? Inside were Elizabeth Barrett and her sisters Arabella and Henrietta, six brothers and five servants. This did not leave much room for their belongings and Elizabeth was only allowed one box of precious books, some of them treasured editions of the classics, gifts from her scholar friend Hugh Stuart Boyd.

Did she look back at the strange Moorish house with its domes and minarets, stained glass and engraved suns and moons set in its valley garden, all trees and rocks and water about which she had scrambled as a child and walked as a girl and which had been such a dearly loved home? Later, she said vehemently she could not bear to return — 'I would as soon open a coffin as do it' — as though it was something hallowed. Even more poignantly, she says of the Malvern Hills in a letter from Wimpole Street, 'And yet not for the whole world's beauty would I stand among the sunshine and shadow of them any more; it would be a mockery, like the taking back of a broken flower to its stalk'.

The mansion, 'the faery palace', which her father Edward Moulton Barrett built in 1809, has gone, demolished in 1872, but the original house on the estate, turned by Barrett into his stable block, remains. It is girdled by its two courtyards and graced by minaret and ogee topped columns. The clocktower, built to the scale of the grand

9

mansion before it, which is celebrated in a charming and graphic little poem by Elizabeth aged nine, still towers over our low brick house. The clockfaces missing from the round windows are reputed to be in Jamaica. The weight no longer rises in its side tower and it is left to the imagination to hear the regular hourly chime of the clock echoing across the cobbled stable yard above the clatter of the horses' hoofs and floating through the valley. The minaret rises from the high wall in the rear courtyard from a thicket of red and white roses, and the ogee columns which once flanked the house support clematis, guelder rose and jasmine. Here in the gardens flourish the acacias, beech, lime, oak and ash, maples and cedars, Portuguese laurels and ancient Spanish chestnuts mentioned by Elizabeth who so often refers to trees, greenness and the green shade cast by trees. Here in the grounds is the ice house where she sat and talked and the high brick walls of the old walled garden. Here too are the rough lime-stone rockfaces, the woodland paths, the bare hilltop with views to the Malvern and Welsh hills. Springs well out of the hillside, the steeply slanting valleys lead down to the long ribbon of water cunningly contrived to look like a small lazy river and the quiet lily pools where the mallard nest.

The lodge and school room still lie at the west entrance and beyond them the home farm oversees the orchards and farms of Hereford-shire stretching out to Wales. The little hexagonal lodge house remains, guarding the south end of the drive facing the whole range of the Malvern Hills, looking over to Barton Court. It stands a mile from Colwall Church where the Barretts' children were christened in groups of three. This is the way Elizabeth would have set out on her forays over the hills to see Hugh Stuart Boyd.

Throughout Elizabeth's writing there are constant reminders of her sense of this place where I now live. In the earliest poems written at Hope End to celebrate her father's birthday and to commemorate the setting up of the clock in the stable yard, Elizabeth describes the immediate world around her with the short focus of a child:

> These polished walls, raised by your tasteful hand,
> These smiling shrubs, these tangled walks and hills,
> These rising rocks, hewn by your active band,
> And drooping flow'rets washed by murmuring rills:
>
> These waters by your hand are taught to glide,
> And wild ducks strain their soaring wing ...

Elizabeth was obviously very aware from a tender age of the pleasure and fulfilment felt by her adored father in creating this little kingdom or paradise for his large family. The loss of it was a trauma which was reflected and eventually resolved in the course of her poetic life.

In her diary written in 1831-1832 the recent death of her mother, sense of impending sale of Hope End, the uncertainty of the family's future and the probable loss of her intellectual companion Hugh Stuart Boyd who was moving from Ruby Cottage (just over the hill from Hope End), all compound her unhappiness.

Emotional exhaustion was often matched with the physical exhaustion which dogged her after her illness when she was fifteen, but her underlying passionate energy was irrepressible. Often she climbed the steepest parts of the Malvern hills, slipping and sliding down the precipitous slopes only to suffer great fatigue afterwards. The majestic landscape seen from the top of the hills contrasted with the secluded hidden world of Hope End but equally inspired her poetic impulse. From the Wyche she describes the view: 'I looked on each side of the elevated place where I sate. Herefordshire all hill and wood — undulating and broken ground! — Worcestershire throwing out a grand unbroken extent, — and more Worcestershire to the horizon! One prospect attracting to the eye, by picturesqueness; the other the mind, — by sublimity'. The balance between the eye and the senses and the mind and intellect is always present in her poetry though perhaps not always recognised in such a cerebral poet. One is constantly delighted and amazed at her sensitivity to physical sensations, the wind in her hair, the moss beneath her feet. August 20th 1831: 'The moon was shining exquisitely, one star by its side, before I left the open air'.

Recalling in her poems the gardens of Hope End and the landscape of the countryside around, from a distance and eventually from a space of twenty five years, when she was writing *Aurora Leigh* the vividness of detail is striking.

'The Deserted Garden', 'The Lost Bower' and 'Hector in the Garden' weave together the theme of the recollection and loss of childhood happiness and the passing of time with all the brilliant clarity of a child's perception. 'The Deserted Garden' recalls the child's blissful pleasure in the beauty of the rosetree wall of the garden — 'earth's greenest place' and her own secret discovery. The strange, almost mystical experience of 'The Lost Bower' when, alone, she discovers a magical place in the woods, is described with precise topographical detail, sweeping up the steep wooded valley sides, then down to the flowers at her feet, lifting her head to the sound of the sheep cropping the grass, observing the quincunx of apple trees casting their shadows to the ground and looking back up to the further hills beyond. And in 'Hector in the Garden' which is openly autobiographical she again describes herself as a child of nine enjoying the simple carefree pleasures of country life.

Descriptions of gardens, parkland and countryside, idyllic picturesque landscapes, draw directly on Elizabeth's childhood memories of Hope End. In 'Lady Geraldine's Courtship' the music from the house floats through the gardens of Wycombe Hall on summer evenings.

> And evermore there was music both of
>   instrument and singing,
> Till the finches of the shrubberies grew
>   restless in the dark;
> But the cedars stood up motionless,
>   each in a moon ringing,
> And the deer, half in the glimmer,
>   strewed the hollows of the park.

But it is in the descriptions of Leigh Hall and its surroundings in *Aurora Leigh* that Elizabeth finally allows herself to recall her Hope End childhood with most clarity, tenderness and familiarity of observation.

On Saturday 11 June 1832 Elizabeth's brother Sam told her that Hope End was advertised for sale in the *Sun* newspaper. Later that day she walked in the garden with her aunt Bummy and sister Arabel on the bank on the far side of the water. The path is still there winding between wild roses and under the acacias. She says in her diary 'Hope is all in vain. We shall leave this place and all that is dear, in it and near it'.

Afterward she told Miss Mitford, 'Even now I never say "Hope End" before him. He loved the place so' ... 'It is a beautiful place — and people crowded to see it under the pretence of purchasing — and our old, serene green stillness was trodden underfoot, day after day' ... 'It was a miserable time ... But in proportion to what has happened since, I do call it a happy time — thrice happy and blessed'.

Almost all who have lived here and visited here have felt this charisma and fallen under its spell. Today, to come over the brow of the hill and drop down into the little valley surrounded completely by a wooded rim is to enter another realm. The outside world drops away. People often remark that they can 'hear the silence'. The tranquillity is palpable, it is not just an absence of noise and bustle. To step outside the door each morning confirms this feeling. In fact, the valley is full of sweet noises and movement. In spring the dawn and evening chorus fills the air as does the hum and murmur of insects in a lower key during the long summer afternoons when the breeze ruffles the wild flowers and meadow grasses. In winter the gales roar high above the rearing heads of the great trees. One listens for the skyline at daybreak to see if the familiar outline has changed. In thunderstorms the lightning seems attracted to the redwood tops and echoes double back from the valley sides and cliffs.

There are the moments we love to mark when the seasons change: the first snowdrops, the sowing of the seeds in the greenhouse, their germination and planting out in the warm hospitable garden, the smell of the first cut of grass, the anxiously awaited arrival of the swallows and house martens and the first flight of their broods, the first strawberries, peas and new potatoes, the cherries, raspberries, figs, melons and pumpkins, apples and pears. Each a new delight. As the leaves float down new vistas and shapes appear, the perspectives lengthen and alter, the light strikes differently, surprisingly, on temple or belvedere or on the detail of the urns, gleaming new when we put them up, now coloured with lichen and mosses, the perch of the robin and wren and, one bright night, an owl.

In winter the steep drive to the north of the house can be sealed with snow for weeks. The cedars of Lebanon are bowed down; sometimes a vast, flat bough breaks under the white weight. Once we found a wild bees' nest amongst the splintered wood. What honey, fragrant with cedar! The logs we burn are cedar, walnut and apple — the heady aromatic scents of summer. Badgers and foxes tunnel beneath the roots of the larger firs and oaks, the ravens roost in their tops. In the walled garden the fruit tree trunks continue to expand during the winter, the buds develop and now the valley, always the same, changes again. It is an incomparable place to live.

— Patricia Hegarty
Hope End, Ledbury, April 1994

One:
Background and Family at Hope End

Not many people associate Elizabeth Barrett Browning with the border country of Wales. Quite other areas have dominated the popular story of her life. Places have always been an important part of the Browning myth, ever since Rudolf Besier fixed the Barrett family forever as the Barretts of Wimpole Street in 1930. It was there in Marylebone that Mr Barrett, Besier's pantomime villain of a Victorian father, imprisoned his terrified children (according to the play), adult as they were, for Elizabeth, the eldest, was nearly forty, and her youngest brother, Octavius, was not much short of twenty. Elizabeth, already widely recognised for the poetry which had appeared in collected form in 1844, was known all over literary London as the ethereal, fragile, reclusive 'invalid of Wimpole Street'. Robert Browning, her secret lover, challenged patriarchal autocracy when he carried her away to a secret marriage and a new life in Florence — and from her dramatic escape in 1846 to her death in 1861 her locale was Italy, and her home at Casa Guidi was as famous as 50 Wimpole Street had ever been.

But for nearly half her life Elizabeth Barrett lived in Herefordshire. Until they moved to London in 1835 'home' was the house near Ledbury, the mansion of 'Indian Gothic' magnificence which her father built in 1809. The locale where her childhood liking for poetry sharpened to a passion (as she put it herself later in a letter to R.H. Horne, 'the early fancy turned into a will, and remained with me — and from that day to this, poetry has been a distinct object ... to read, think, and live for', [LRH, 154]), and her childish verses developed to the mature work of a poet recognised nationally, was the Malvern Hills. Long after the family had joined the swelling population of London, she looked back with sick regret at the hills and trees of

Herefordshire — 'How often my thoughts are at home!', she said sadly to a friend, 'I cannot help calling it so still in my thoughts' (L, 1, 27 September 1832), and her poems recapture the details of her childhood experience there.

It is time to redefine the significance of locale in the life and work of a poet who, as Elizabeth Barrett Browning, was compared seriously with Shakespeare, and this has been my aim here. Many books have been written recently on the poet who became famous in London and then in Florence, but little has been written on the early years when her potential first became apparent and her genius began to show. All the sources of her inspiration were at Hope End, and to the end their influence is discernible. Her married name will be used sparingly in the account which follows. The name by which the world knew her then, first in Herefordshire and then in London, was Elizabeth Barrett — and her family called her not 'Elizabeth' but 'Ba'. It has seemed appropriate to refer to her throughout this account by either her first professional name, or (according to the context) by the less familiar form of her family name, 'Elizabeth'.

When Wordsworth, the Poet Laureate, died in 1850 there was a strong and influential body of opinion which urged that the time had come to break with the tradition of centuries in the appointment of his successor, and that the post which had been held from the time of Dryden by a man should now be offered to a woman. The British throne was occupied by a woman, and a queen ruled the greatest empire in history. Would it not be appropriate, suggested the *Athenaeum*, for the Laureateship to be offered to the greatest living poet of the time, to Mrs Browning? Not to Robert Browning, of course: he still had his name to make, and was at that time a largely unheard-of scribbler who lived in Florence, known by a few as a young poet only notable for his wilful obscurity. But his wife's poetic reputation, which had blossomed before they left England, was at its height. Her famous *Sonnets from the Portuguese* had just appeared in the first collected edition of her poetry, and the *Athenaeum* called her, triumphantly, 'of her sex, the most imaginative writer England has produced in any age'. It spoke admiringly of her electric passion, her noble thought, and her bold yet delicate imagination. Robert Browning, in the same number, was dismissed as a writer of doggerel verse, whose 'coarse and grotesque' writing it found offensive and odd. His wife was always his firmest supporter (she had made the first overtures between them when she referred to his poetry enthusiastically in an earlier volume of poetry in 1844), but even she had no thoughts of him as the Laureate. The position was in fact offered to Tennyson, whose *In Memoriam* was published in the same month as the *Athenaeum* article, and it was a decision with which the unsuccessful candidate heartily concurred.

Elizabeth Barrett had left England as a secret bride in 1846, but her reputation as a poet had grown steadily in the intervening years, and her position in English poetry was, it seemed, established. Her success was not unlooked for. All her life she had been conscious of her position as a Poet (and not merely a poetess), and accepted fame as the natural corollary of her ambition. Indeed the Laureateship was an honour she had already been offered in another context. At four years old, she tells us in an autobiographical fragment written at fourteen,

> I first mounted Pegasus, but at six I thought myself privileged
> to show off feats of horsemanship.
> (*Autobiographical Essays*, 349)

She had been writing verses ever since she could hold a pen, annually producing birthday odes for each member of the family; and with the greatest care, we are told, she wrote a poem on Virtue 'in her sixth year'. For this she received from her father a ten-shilling note in a letter solemnly addressed to 'the Poet Laureate of Hope End'. And never could a gesture have pleased her more, for, she adds, 'I received much more pleasure from the word Poet than from the ten-shilling note' (*Autobiographical Essays*, 350).

Elizabeth Barrett Browning came from a very wealthy family. Her father, Edward Moulton Barrett, was the younger son of a slave-owning family with sugar plantations in the West Indies, the co-inheritor of his grandfather's sugar estates. He had been sent to England in 1792 at the age of seven to go to Harrow and then Cambridge, and had stayed to marry the daughter of a similar family in Newcastle, Mary Graham-Clarke. He had spent his holidays there throughout his school and college days, and Mary was, we gather, the object of his first, his earliest, and his only affections. Mary was a few years older than Edward, who was very young indeed, but was in no doubt where her choice lay.

The approval of the match from the older generation was delayed only until Edward's guardian in England, acting for parents in the

West Indies, had actually met his ward's intended, when he declared, 'I hold out no longer — she is far too good for him!' (LS, vii). They were married in May 1805, and stayed for a time in the north-east, near Mary Graham-Clarke's family: they rented the imposing Coxhoe Hall near Durham, and there, eleven months after the wedding, Elizabeth was born on 6 March 1806.

Now that he was the father of a family, young Edward (he was still just short of twenty-one when Elizabeth was born) began to think seriously of a permanent home of his own, and made long journeys to investigate possible sites in different parts of the country. He was conscious of financial concern and the threat of pressure (it was a time of anxious waiting in the sugar trade — generally, as the industry moved towards its own time of crisis, as the question of Abolition assumed a definite form, and more particularly on the Moulton Barrett estate after the death of Edward's grandfather, and a disputed will), and he was acting on his father's behalf in London.

His first son, Edward, was born, fifteen months after Elizabeth, before he found the place he was looking for. It was in Herefordshire, the county where his wife's brother had already settled; it was near Ledbury, and had the unpromising name of 'Hope End' (which was merely 'a closed valley'). Here he planned and built a mansion which was an oriental extravaganza, and here were born the rest of his large family. They were twelve in all. Henrietta was born some weeks before they arrived there (via Surrey) in 1809, Mary (who died aged four) in 1810, Samuel in 1812, Arabella in 1813; and after them six more boys between 1814 and 1826. Most as well as baptismal names had nicknames: Elizabeth herself was 'Ba', and Edward 'Bro'. Henrietta was 'Daddles', and Arabella 'Arabel'. Alfred was 'Daisy', Charles was 'Stormie', Octavius and Septimus were predictably 'Occy' and 'Setty'.

To Elizabeth the most important of them all was Edward, scarcely more than a year the younger. Throughout their childhood Bro was her constant and loved companion with whom she shared everything: interests, pleasures, affections, and in the earliest years, education. Elizabeth's feelings for him were summed up in the autobiographical fragment:

> If ever I loved any human being, I love this dear Brother ... the partner of the pleasures of my literary toils. My attachment to him is literally devoted.
> (*Autobiographical Essays*, 354)

Her feelings for her other siblings were always warm, but were never expressed on the passionate terms reserved for Bro. Henrietta was the sister closest to her in age, and as adults they were always on excellent terms; but Henrietta as a girl was always too close to what Elizabeth despised as the superficialities of social convention to be a real companion, and seems indeed to have had little of the qualities Elizabeth saw in Bro or herself. Arabel, too young to be a regular companion, was all the same very much more on Elizabeth's wavelength than the bubbly Henrietta. Arabel at eighteen was, noted Elizabeth,

> an interesting, intelligent, amiable, feeling girl. I should love her even if she were not my sister;

whereas she wished that the unfortunate Henrietta

> would estimate people more by their minds than she actually does ... and that she were not so fond of visiting for visiting's sake.
> (*Diary*, 42, 182)

Occy and Setty, from whom she was divided by almost a generation, she mothered and adored ('Dearest Occyta playing with me all the evening, I do love him!' [*Diary*, 203]. 'Sette to Worcester [to the dentist]. Five tugs, and Sette's tooth — and he did not cry!' [*Diary*, 219]). She taught the younger boys Latin and Greek in their preparation for school; but Charles ('Stormie'), George, Henry and Alfred were perforce less distinct — though on their birthdays each had a separate ode from Elizabeth.

As for the parents, there was never any question as to who held sway over the community at Hope End, or who demanded and received the unquestioning loyalty, obedience, and love of the young family. For Elizabeth it was her father, Edward Moulton Barrett, who was at the centre of her life. Their relationship was characterised in her childhood by uncritical adoration on her side, and on his by indulgent affection and admiration. In the early years he was generous with both time and money. He encouraged Elizabeth's writing, he funded all the expenses of *The Battle of Marathon* in 1820, and was delighted with her success when it came. He permitted all his children an unexpected degree of familiarity ('Puppy' was the name he enjoyed in the family), and they all in later life confirm the happiness of their childhood and their deep love of their father. The image of the Victorian ogre of Wimpole Street who repressed and terrified his grown children came later. At Hope End though he represented authority he was a playful companion too.

Elizabeth's feelings for both her parents were deeply loving. Her father was the more forceful, perhaps, in all the different areas of the partnership, but both parents were equally involved in their daughter's vocation, and shared their pride in her achievements. When Elizabeth's first success, her 'Lines on the Death of Lord Byron' appeared anonymously in the *Globe and Traveller* in June 1824, Mary Moulton Barrett, who knew the secret, asked her husband with seeming casualness what he thought of the 'Lines' for

> 'I cannot help thinking ... that we know something of the author.'
> 'They cannot be Ba's', said he, taking the paper from me to read it again, 'though certainly when I first read them they reminded me greatly of her style — have you any idea they are hers?'
> 'I have a *conviction* of it' said the conceited mother, pouring out the tea.
> (*The Brownings' Correspondence*, 1, 198)

When *An Essay on Mind* appeared two years later Mary Moulton Barrett declared,

> There never was any circumstance, in the existence of your dearest Father or my own, that could afford us the same gratified feelings, as this strong evidence that our beloved child has so well applied and cultivated the talents with which she is gifted.
> (Ibid, 237)

Elizabeth loved her mother deeply, and suffered her unexpected death at forty-seven, in 1828, as a devastating blow ('Do I not feel now bitterly, desolately, that human love like hers I never can find again!' she wrote broodingly in her diary in 1831). All the same, she did not see Mary Moulton Barrett as a role model. Her mother had complied with every expectation of a well-born girl in most ages: that she marry early, to the best advantage, and bear children; and in her twenty-two years of marriage there had been few when she had not been involved in the birth and rearing of her twelve children.

Elizabeth had quite other plans for her life, and her worst nightmare when she was twenty-five was that of marriage:

> I dreamt last night that I was married ... and in an agony to procure a dissolution of the engagement. Scarcely ever considered my single state with more satisfaction than when I awoke!
> (*Diary*, 111)

Her father's notorious later refusal to admit even thoughts of marriage for any of his children (whether his wife would have meekly concurred with his chilling edict we can only conjecture) had not yet arisen, but Elizabeth's own scorn for the young men who from time to time appeared in the area was sufficient to deter any overtures.

For Elizabeth was single-minded in considering her vocation. Her life was to be given to poetry, and no competition from personal feeling was to be admitted even as a possibility. Her life was not to be spent as her mother's had been spent, always in the shadow of her husband. She was ruefully conscious of the absence of women from the canon of literature, and was determined that no pressures from society should prevent her from achieving what she felt she had been sent into the world to do. She wrote famously to Mr Chorley at the *Athenaeum* later,

> It is a strong impression with me that previous to Joanna Baillie [1762-1851; a popular Scottish writer and playwright] there was no such thing in England as a poetess ... I look everywhere for grandmothers and see none ... England has had many learned women, not merely readers but writers of the learned languages, and yet where were the poetesses?
> (L, 1, 3 January 1845)

Her mother's life, dear and cherished though it had been, was a warning to her that there were choices to be made, and made with care.

She was to discover, of course, that no such choice would be necessary, that her conscious pride in the acknowledged position as 'of her sex the most imaginative writer England has produced in any age' would be triumphantly combined with the role of wife and mother. But that came later. Until Elizabeth verged on middle age it seemed to the world that the Laureate of Hope End had embraced that calling, and in her move to London had merely become the invalid of Wimpole Street, perhaps Poet Laureate-in-waiting.

* * *

Edward Barrett bought his estate in Herefordshire in 1809 from neighbouring landowners in Northumberland, in a part of the country deliberately remote from his in-laws and from the house near Durham where Elizabeth had been born, and made it uniquely his own. It was three miles from Ledbury and four from Malvern. The house was set in more than four hundred and seventy acres of ground, and was called Hope End. Edward Barrett decided on the spot to change it all, and build his own house in a fantasy vision of oriental magnificence.

The timing of his decision is interesting and significant, for his vision for Hope End is not unique. The brief style of architecture that came to be known as 'Indian Gothic' had recently made its appearance. The most famous example is the Brighton Pavilion, which was begun for the Prince Regent in 1804 and finished some years later by Nash. The Prince had made similar experiments in his town house: in the redecorating of Carlton House, the personal residence given to him when he came of age in 1783, the Prince Regent had spent twenty-five years creating a riot of Gothic pinnacles, Chinese dragons, and Egyptian sphinxes, with a wide use of brass and metal inlay. Edward Barrett's taste was princely, in fact, in every sense.

The earliest example of 'Indian Gothic', however, anticipates Brighton Pavilion by a year, and is at Sezincote in Gloucestershire, where S.P. Cockerell, Nash's pupil, built a house similar to Hope End for his retired 'Indian Nabob' brother, not too far from the corner of Herefordshire which Edward Barrett had selected. It seems likely that Barrett saw this remarkable building on his frequent forays in search of a house. The design of the house at Hope End was his own, and it became a showpiece for the county as it rose over the next six years. His son George speculated much later that the architect was 'Wyatt', presumably the James Wyatt who built the equally spectacular Fonthill for William Beckford in the early years of the century. George was probably right. Wyatt (1746-1813) was the great Gothic architect of the time before Gothic became consciously archaeological, and Fonthill, the brainchild of another eccentric even richer than Barrett, was his most wonderfully bizarre secular building, and had much in common with Hope End. Fonthill was a paradigm of all the characteristics of eighteenth century romantic Gothic, and though it probably included no traces of 'Indian Gothic' fantasy, as Kenneth Clarke declared 'Fonthill always appealed primarily to the imagination, was always an Arabian Nights' dream' (Kenneth Clarke, *The Gothic Revival*, 72), and was, in fact, even more evanescent than Hope End.

Hope End assumed the form of what his wife described as out of 'the Arabian Nights tales', with a dome and minarets and ogee-headed windows outside. Inside no detail was too insignificant for the imagination of the designer. The Sale Catalogue of some twenty-five years later offers some details. The doors were satinwood or mahogany inlaid with mother-of-pearl, the balustrades of 'the noble principal stone staircase' in the hall were brass, the walls of the morning-room were 'handsomely stuccoed and painted', the dining-room was papered in crimson flock, the drawing-room was 'thirty-six feet by twenty-one feet with circular end', with 'beautiful marble chimney-piece, richly ornamented with ormulu'. Every surface was decorated with 'Turkish views' or ornamented in 'the Chinese style', and the Gothic windows were filled with stained glass. Everything, Mary Barrett told her mother, was 'unique and striking' (*Diary*, xv).

While the house was under construction the new owner employed a celebrated landscape-gardener, John Claudius Loudon, to lay out the grounds. (This at any rate was the emphatic opinion of George.) A subterranean passage led the visitor from the house to 'Extensive Gravelled Walks through a Shrubbery,' and lawns, woods, and a lake. 'There are deer in the park', wrote Mary Barrett, 'and it is surrounded with fine hills covered with wood. A stream runs through it — forming a cascade. Nothing in short ever was so picturesque and beautiful!' (*Diary*, xv).

If George was right, and Loudon did indeed landscape the park at Hope End, then Edward Barrett showed remarkable prescience, for Loudon was at the beginning of his career when the estate was bought in 1809, and much involved in projects elsewhere. Whether he laid out the grounds or not, Edward had still selected a remarkable enough corner of Herefordshire for his own experiments in design, for Uvedale Price lived nearby at Foxley, and Richard Payne Knight not much further away at Downton Castle, and both were major contributors to the theories of picturesque design in architecture and gardens. Both must have viewed the progress of Hope End, house and park, with great interest.

It was no wonder that the fairy-tale palace and its surrounding estate should attract the observation of the curious, or indeed that the extravagance and flamboyance of such an architectural style should be captured by the satirists. Maria Edgeworth's novel *The Absentee Landlord* (1812), written as Hope End was finally reaching completion and already the talk of the county, gives a sly picture of Lady Clonbrony's fashionable new ballroom which reads like a house-agent's catalogue of Hope End. Lady Clonbrony's designer, a very successful Regency entrepreneur, urges her to

> round your walls with the Turkish tent drapery — in apricot cloth, or crimson velvet ... and for seats here, the SERAGLIO OTTOMANS, superfine scarlet ... For the next apartment, it strikes me — as your la'ship don't value expense — the Alhambra hangings .... Then for the little room, I recommend turning it into a Chinese pagoda with the Chinese pagoda paper, with the porcelain border ... Or, if your la'ship prefers it, the Egyptian Hieroglyphic paper, with the ibis border to match ...
>
> (*The Absentee Landlord*, Ch 2)

Can Maria Edgeworth have heard of Hope End, and seen it on her way from Ireland on the journey from Fishguard? The evidence is alas only circumstantial, though the theory is attractive! Other writers also noticed the development of this kind of architectural phenomenon, and made comments less barbed but as pointed. One, interestingly enough, was Elizabeth's later friend Miss Mitford, who observed a family home with mild dismay in an early number of *Our Village*:

> Every room is in masquerade: the saloon Chinese, full of jars and mandarins and pagodas; the library Egyptian, all covered with hieroglyphics ... They sleep in Turkish tents, and dine in a Gothic chapel.

Little remains of the glory that was Hope End: less than fifty years after the Barretts left, Victorian taste, looking askance at the frivolities of the Regency, with a shudder destroyed it with gunpowder, and built another mansion in a staider form of Gothic. Almost the only evidence we have now of Edward Barrett's vision is in the letters, the watercolours, and the sale catalogue which survive. But in its finest hours Hope End was the nurturer of the genius of Elizabeth Barrett, the home she loved and in which she lived for almost half her life. One of the 'capital bedchambers looking to lawn and water' described by the London estate-agent was the base for her earliest writing, and the estate around was the source for many poems: references to it pervade her work to the end. It was the scene of a number of poems of childhood reminiscence, such as 'Hector in the Garden', 'The Lost Bower', and 'The Deserted Garden'. It meant so much to her for all kinds of reasons, that she could never bear to revisit it later. 'Beautiful, beautiful hills', she wrote to a well-meaning neighbour, Mrs Julia Martin, who pressed her to return:

> and yet not for the whole world of beauty would I stand amongst the sunshine and the shadow of them any more; it would be a mockery, like the taking back of a broken flower to its stalk.
> (L, II, July-August 1855)

The whole area was too much charged with the turbulence of the past and the circumstances of their departure.

'Such a sight! Such a sea of land', she wrote in her diary after an expedition through the Malvern Hills shortly before they left Herefordshire, when she had sat 'on the Worcestershire side' of the pass on the road to Great Malvern ('the view is grand, extensive, and beautiful beyond description' Diary, 135).

> Sublime sight I must still call it! ... I looked on each side of the elevated place where I sat, Herefordshire all hill and wood — undulating and broken ground — Worcestershire throwing out a grand, unbroken extent ... One prospect attracting the eye by picturesqueness, the other the mind — by sublimity.
> (Diary, 7)

The countryside round Hope End was territory she had explored long ago in the years of her greatest impressionability. Here she had enjoyed the tomboyish pleasures of her childhood. She had climbed trees and made slides, and caught fish and romped by the hour with Bro and Sam, and she remembered the happiness and the company made absent through death too poignantly to revisit the scenes.

Years later, possibly to amuse her young Herefordshire cousin, she wrote her experiences down in a story about a girl called 'Beth', a thinly-disguised version of 'Ba' herself.

The unfinished account has as one central concern 'Beth's' adventures with her Shetland pony Moses, who grazes the hills — and who makes more than one appearance in Elizabeth's own diary of 1832. Here in the account for her cousin Lizzie we hear of the anguish that Moses sometimes caused his young mistress who 'best of all liked riding ... galloping till the trees raced past her and the clouds were shot over her head like horizontal arrows from a giant's bow ... leaping over ditches — feeling the live creature beneath her swerve and bound with its own force ... These were great joys for [Ba]!' (*Autobiographical Essays*, 362). But sometimes the pony was stubborn:

> Sometimes Moses was upon the hills, and rejoicing in his liberty refused to be caught ... Beth ... having run until her heart beat and she heard it with her own ears, and her cheeks burnt to scarlet, had to go home with tears running down them, disappointed of her ride, and thinking bitter things of Moses.
> (Ibid.)

The diary also has rueful accounts of Elizabeth's own vain attempts to master the pony. Not always, though:

> At other times, great was the joy thereof. When [Ba] rode on the Malvern Hills, she would leave the rein loose, and Moses would climb the long steeps surefootedly as a goat. He never forgot the tradition of his Shetland.
> (Ibid.)

These were the experiences and memories of childhood, and they were burned deep in her consciousness. Yet the associations with Hope End and the Malvern Hills were as much with her young adult life as her youth. Throughout her diary, kept when she was twenty-five, she writes about the demurer expeditions made with Arabel and Henrietta or 'Bummy', the aunt who spent a long time with them, especially after her mother's death. They made expeditions to pick mushrooms, or to enjoy the countryside on horseback, or simply to visit friends and neighbours like the Biddulphs, the Commelines, the Martins, and the family of Lord Somers at Eastnor

Castle. Time and again she records in her diary, 'How I enjoyed the walking, and the odours of the fresh evening and the sights of the superb and majestic hills':

> I mounted Henrietta's 'high horse'... until we had topped the hill. Glorious hills! How finely they seemed to overlook the great expanse, as if they exalted in their own beauty. But the wind blew away all reverieing!
> (*Diary*, 134)

and she notes her own 'love of silence and quietness, and the sight of the green hills and fields ... '.

Elizabeth had her own reasons too, of course, for valuing the road that led over the hills from Hope End to Great Malvern, for there were all her associations of her visits to Ruby Cottage to see her friend Hugh Boyd. With him she read Greek and discussed religion, and maintained a passionate and irreproachable academic relationship. Or so it seemed to all observers, and the letters between them suggest no other relationship. Only Elizabeth's secret diary, discovered in 1961, a century after her death, offers a different account of what was happening in her mind at this turbulent period, and reveals the progress of an emotionally adolescent young woman as her deepest feelings were first stirred. Every detail of the journey along the road to Boyd's house is recorded. Sometimes the opportunity even to see the tops of Mr Boyd's chimneys is sufficient reason to scramble to the top of the Wyche, and the possible chance of seeing Boyd himself is incentive enough to make a walk with Henrietta a delightful prospect. It is all recorded in the diary, with wit, urbanity, and passion.

But her relationship with Hugh Boyd came late in her life at Hope End, and belongs to a different part of the narrative. It marks the beginning of her adult life. Throughout her childhood and adolescence the focus of her attention was Hope End and the family — she never supposed that life held anything for her outside the context of the house she loved, the 'beautiful, beautiful hills' that surrounded it, and the family she adored.

Two: Education — 'The Steep Ascent'

Outdoors was the time for pleasure and relaxation. Within the house the day revolved, for the children at least, largely round the schoolroom which overlooked the lawn where the boys played cricket.

In an early poem Elizabeth has left a vivid picture of home life at Hope End for the older members of the family (Elizabeth, Bro, Henrietta, Sam, Arabel). Writing when she was thirteen she described the daily routine:

> At school till five! and then again we fly
> To play and joy and mirth and pleasures ply.
> Some dance, some fight, some laugh, some play, some squall
> And the loud organ's thunder circles all.
> And then at tea we snatch a short repast,
> As long as one large plate of toast doth last.
> At nine fatigued upon the grateful bed
> We stretch out weary limbs and rest our head.

Her education, in fact, was not all of the formal kind. Ever the natural leader, she organized plays and tableaux with the others and staged them for a captive audience at Hope End. She compelled each of them to write poems to celebrate birthdays and she read and read right through childhood (particularly novels — she read as many novels as the bookseller could supply. Scott and Edgeworth were favourites in adolescence). But lessons of the formal kind were no problem at all, and she shone at everything she was required to learn.

Education played a serious part in the theories of the Barrett parents, though they were quite relaxed and forward-looking in their interpretation of the term, striving to instil principles as much as information. All the children were taught not to waste their talents, to make the most of opportunities, and to do themselves justice. In the early years Mary Barrett taught the children herself; then she handed the girls over to the governess, the boys to tutors. At the appropriate time the boys departed to school while the girls remained with the governess, Mrs Orme. But the important elementary education of all the children, and the formation of attitudes, was in Mary Barrett's hands. She took the job seriously: one letter sent to her own mother in Newcastle contained a very early exercise of Elizabeth's with the comment, 'This Elegant Scratch you will, I know, be glad to have ... bad and ill-written as it is' (Forster, 16).

When the children were learning French from a French governess later after a visit to France, Mary Barrett adopted methods which would have won high praise from modern educationalists, when she encouraged the children to write to her in French, and maintain a correspondence in the language. Elizabeth Barrett tells us of yet more modern teaching methods and learning experiences when she describes 'Beth's' (her own) relationship with the French poodle Havannah who only understood French:

> Beth's first French was murmured in his ear. The 'Venez-ici' and 'coucher' were next to the 'Baisez-moi' which she climbed upon her father's bed to wake him withal ... That 'Baisez-moi' was lisped against the pillow. She liked that sort of French much better than the French put into verbs, which appeared to her a most atrocious invention — most probably Boney's own.
>
> (*Autobiographical Essays*, 362)

In 1815, when Elizabeth was nine, her father, acting on his own principles of never wasting an opportunity, made the very enterprising decision to take the family to Paris, accessible at the end of the Revolutionary Wars for the first time in twenty years. So Elizabeth became conscious of a foreign language in the proper context, and she improved her French still further when she spent six months in Boulogne some years later.

Meanwhile, other languages attracted her which were beyond her mother's skills, and well outside the conventions of the normal education for girls. Bro had begun his preparations for Charterhouse with a tutor, Mr McSwiney. 'At eleven,' Elizabeth declares in *Glimpses of my Own Life and Literary Character*, 'I felt the most ardent desire to understand the learned languages. To comprehend even the Greek alphabet was delight inexpressible. Under the tuition of

Mr McSwiney I attained that which I most fervently desired' (*Autobiographical Essays*, 350). At eleven she had cried 'very heartily for half an hour' (ibid.) because she did not understand Greek: with the benefit of Mr McSwiney's instruction she confesses 'to be a good linguist is the height of my ambition and I do not believe that I can ever cease desiring to attain this!' (ibid., 355). It is part of the vow she has made to herself, 'never to pause at undertaking any literary difficulty if convinced of its final utility' (ibid.). Now she can read 'Homer in the original with delight inexpressible, together with Vergil' (ibid.), and one end is achieved.

It does not seem that Bro, with whom she shared everything ('Our minds, souls, are united by the same opinions, the same interests!' ... 'the partner of my pleasures of my literary toils', [*Autobiographical Essays*, 354]), was quite at one with her in her passion for classical learning. She said of him herself, in an essay she wrote on *My Character and Bro's Compared*, that while her drive was always to excel, 'Bro is satisfied with mediocrity. He possesses too much humility to soar, and therefore stoops lower than is necessary' (*Autobiographical Essays*, 357). His career at Charterhouse was quite undistinguished. Yet it was Bro who — automatically — followed the path of all boys of his age and station and went away to school to enjoy the education his sister cried for in vain.

It was a situation familiar to many young bluestockings. Two famous ones in fiction illustrate Elizabeth's plight: Maggie Tulliver in *The Mill on the Floss*, gifted far beyond her sullen brother Tom, watches him in tantalised dismay throw away his chance of education at school; and in Charlotte Yonge's *The Daisy Chain*, a bestseller of 1856, Ethel May is determined not to fall behind her brother Norman in composing Latin verses when he enters for the Stoneborough scholarship at Oxford from his school, and only concedes the goal when persuaded by her adored father that her ambition is unwomanly, and she must fulfil her role at home. For there were no schools for ambitious girls to rival Charterhouse (or Stoneborough). Until much later in the century the best to be hoped for, if you were a clever girl, seemed to be the conscientious teaching of parents, or a good governess, or the occasional share of a brother's tutor. Bro's letters from Charterhouse urging the brutality of the regime, or the scantiness of the diet, or the appalling bullying, brought little comfort to his frustrated sister.

Bro's fortune must have provoked rank envy in Elizabeth. At

Hope End education for the girls in the family was not a serious issue. After Mary Barrett's initial instruction, the girls had the benefit of (sporadic) governesses from whom they learned or not, largely as they chose. Mr McSwiney left Hope End when Bro went to Charterhouse, and from the age of fourteen Elizabeth was almost entirely self-educated. Given her poor health and the long periods spent away from Hope End (during her illnesses, for example, or when she was able to be in France, or on long visits to relatives with her family), it could hardly have been otherwise. She had occasional help from Mr McSwiney when Bro forwarded her exercises for his attention, or passed on his old tutor's advice after he had seen him in London, but in the main her 'steep ascent towards the bright pinnacle of learning' was a lonely one.

Her achievement — in any circumstances, but in these in particular — is quite remarkable. Before she left Hope End, when she was twenty-six, she had finished a translation of Aeschylus' *Prometheus Bound*, which was published with early poems in 1833. Further translations from Bion, Theocritus, Apuleius, Hesiod, Homer and others followed in later volumes. One of the titles she wanted to possess in 1824 (we know from her notebook) was an essay on the genius and writing of Homer; and the extent of her reading with Hugh Boyd is awesome. 'I intend to give up Greek when I give up poetry', she had written to him in 1830.

What is also awesome is her parents' total lack of real sympathy with or understanding of her situation. There is no evidence at all that Edward and Mary Barrett, proud as they were of their daughter and largely sympathetic to her ambitions, ever made any attempt to find an answer to her problems, or to procure the help she needed. There is no question that her father could have afforded a tutor, had he been prepared to take her yearnings seriously. But to the end of her life Elizabeth was ruefully conscious of the gaps in her education, and angry at the unnecessary disadvantages under which she (and other women) laboured. Speaking as 'Beth', her alter ego, she tells us of her childhood ambitions for fame, for glory, for martial eminence. But, says the author, 'Poor Beth had one misfortune. She was born a woman'. So even her other ambition — to be a poet ('there was the reigning thought') — is a dream.

> No woman was ever before such a poet as she would be. As Homer was among men, so she would be among women —

she would be the feminine of Homer ... When she grew up she
would wear men's clothes, and live on a Greek island ... [and]
she would teach the islanders the ancient Greek, and they
would all talk there of the old glories in the real Greek
sunshine, with the right ais and ois ...
(*Autobiographical Essays*, 361)

Elizabeth had so far followed 'Beth's' prescription, then, in that she
had early begun to make her name as both a scholar and a poet, and
had her father's approval for both. While she was 'the Poet Laureate
of Hope End', in fact, she had his whole admiration and approbation.
For 'the poet at his knee' ('The Pet-Name') any indulgence was
appropriate except a formal education. Only when she left this
defined domain did their relationship show any hint of strain, and
that mainly after her mother's death. Edward Barrett's own education had been irregular, and rather limited. He had been sent back
from the West Indies as a small boy to be educated in England, and
had spent some years with a tutor before going briefly to Harrow
(he was withdrawn after rebelling against the system which required him to act as a fag) at twelve. But most of his education was
at home until he went (again briefly) to Cambridge, which he left
without taking a degree — and he was married at twenty.

His own deficiencies in education, however, brought him no clear
perception of his duties to his remarkable daughter, and throughout
the time of her growing fame — until Robert Browning challenged
his authority, in fact — he saw himself as her obvious point of
reference and most valuable critic. Though on the surface Elizabeth
accepted the authority he assumed, there are growing signs that she
was beginning to question it. A minor crisis came in February 1827,
when she showed him a poem on which she had been working for
months. He received it with a coldness and discouragement that she
found quite dismaying, and he compounded his cruelty with a
dismissal she found hurtful beyond words:

'You see the subject [the development of genius] is beyond
your grasp — and you must be content with what you can
reach ... I advise you to burn the wretched thing.'
Thus was I dismissed after months of anxious solitary
thought, after months of apprehension mingled with rejoicing
expectation. I did not say a word: it was harder to prevent
myself from shedding a tear ... I have hardly ever been mor-

tified as I was mortified last night ... Papa's expression 'that my subject was beyond my grasp', lets me see at once how limited he considers my talents. I believe I did not consider my talents so limited, and I certainly did not know that he thought so ... I cannot give up completing the poem I was advised to burn ...

(*Autobiographical Essays*, 359-60)

Certainly the implication is there, in the brooding account she wrote in her distress, that she had begun to concede the possibility of flaws in her father's sensibility; and the poem was finished, though not published until after her death.

Edward Barrett's sympathy with her ambitions extended only as far as his own imagination, and beyond that it stopped. As long as she presented him with no competition his encouragement was unstinting. But when she surpassed his limitations and challenged his self-appointed position, she could not, we see, look to him for the support she had taken for granted.

Elizabeth Barrett's life, as the eldest of the tight little community at Hope End, is inevitably very much bound up with her father's at this stage. She was almost tunnel-visioned in her pursuit of her vocation, and except where her perceptions and his collided directly (as in the question of her education and his reception of her poetry) she seems to have been happy to accept his views without demur. The myth of Elizabeth and her father is due mostly to the imagination of later romancers eager for the material of melodrama, and the picture that emerges from the diary and letters of Hope End days is different from that recorded of Wimpole Street especially as notoriously interpreted by Rudolph Besier. The relationship between them in the early days was mostly happy and unstrained, as with all his children. Although he demanded unquestioning obedience from them, within his own terms and theirs he was kindly, thoughtful, and companionable. Elizabeth's accounts in her diary of family activities like cricket with the boys, and theatricals, and shooting expeditions, all suggest a very different personality from the one passed down by legend.

The darker side of Edward Barrett's nature became more apparent after his wife's death in 1828 and the years following. They were sombre years for the Barretts: all the news from the West Indies was bad as the financial fortunes involved in the plantations threatened to topple with Abolition. The lawsuit which followed a disputed inheritance ended disastrously for the Barretts in Jamaica, and the financial implications were grievous for the family in Herefordshire. The fate of Hope End hung in the balance. The religious melancholia to which Edward Barrett had always been prone settled on him now, without the cheerfulness and even temper of his wife to support him.

In the years which followed his wife's death Elizabeth was the main emotional support to whom he turned for companionship and solace. It was a relationship of mutual dependence. The year in which she kept a diary was the crisis year for Hope End, and Edward Barrett spent much of it in London, desperately trying to straighten out the problems of enormous wealth and summon enough to rescue the estate. He felt he could not share the burden with anybody, and Elizabeth's loneliness and distress in the diary are marked. When the crash came and Hope End had to be sold, Elizabeth's concern is as much on his behalf as on her own. (Ten years later she wrote to Miss Mitford, 'How I remember the coming of the letter to apprise him of the loss of his fortune ... Even now I never say 'Hope End' before him. He loved the place so ...' [LM, 6 December 1842].)

Later, in the haven of Wimpole Street Edward Barrett was a constant companion and friend in the sickroom which became her home after the apparent onset of tubercular disease, and the relationship between the father and his eldest child intensified. 'He is so kind, so tender ... ' she told Miss Mitford. 'No love of mine can echo back his as far as demonstration goes — I love him inwardly, I was going to say better than my life' (LM, 14 June 1841), and we know it was his custom to pray with her there nightly.

Emotionally Edward Barrett fulfilled all her needs as she recognised them in Wimpole Street. He was to continue to do so until the appearance of Robert Browning released all her potential and need for an adult relationship. Intellectually she had outgrown his limitations long before they left Hope End. Hugh Boyd, himself limited in achieving the goals he could suggest, had replaced her father as the ultimate arbiter in things academic, and represented the nearest she got to a formal teacher; and she acknowledged him gratefully. In terms of poetry nobody at Hope End, neither Edward Barrett nor Hugh Boyd, could give her what she asked for — sympathy which was both instinctive and informed — and in that too Browning was her perfect tutor.

The movement of Elizabeth Barrett's mind and her growth as a poet, from when at four she 'mounted Pegasus' and became at six the Laureate of Hope End, to her recognition by the world as the foremost poet of the time, is all recorded in her 'novel in verse', *Aurora Leigh*. The early books are witness to the Hope End years, the crucial period when Elizabeth Barrett was defining herself as a poet and testing the water of critical reception.

The story of the young Aurora Leigh as recorded by the poet is in many respects a version of the story of the young Elizabeth Barrett. Aurora, born in Italy of a Tuscan mother and an English father, loses her mother when barely more than a baby, and her father as she enters adolescence, and she begins her life as an artist quite alone, among people who cannot understand her. On her father's death she is sent back from the warmth and vitality of Italy to England, an unwelcoming foreign land. She arrives in London to 'find a house/Among those mean red houses through the fog' (I, 252-3), to be brought up by her maiden aunt in a country house on the borders of Wales. Her aunt, though coldly kind, has no real sympathy for the child, having always lived 'A quiet life, which was no life at all/(But that, she had not lived enough to know), /Between the vicar and the country squires' (I, 289-91), and she educates her niece with rigid conventionality, 'Because she owned she liked accomplishments in girls' (I, 426) — 'she owned/She liked a woman to be womanly' (I, 442-3).

Aurora in silent despair obeys, and labours at the arts of sketching and the polka and even masters cross-stitch. But she knows that she is different, that there should be more to her life than her aunt's, which is that of a caged bird. After a time of dumb submission ('There seemed more true life in my father's grave/Than in all England', [I, 375-6]) in her little chamber in the house, possible avenues of escape offer themselves. She starts to

> ... escape
> As a soul from a body, out of doors,
> Glide through the shrubberies, drop into the lane,
> And wander on the hills an hour or two,
> Then back again before the house should stir.
>   (I, 693-7)

Alternatively, she makes the most of the solitude of her own room:

> I sat on in my chamber green,
> And thought my thoughts, and prayed

> My prayers without the vicar ...
>   (I, 698-700)

She falls back on what she had learned from her father in her motherless life in Italy:

> I read much. What my father taught before
> From many a volume ... the trick of Greek
> And Latin he had taught me, as he would
> Have taught me wrestling or the game of fives
> If such he had known ...
> He wrapt his daughter in his large
> Man's doublet, careless did it fit or no.
>   (I, 710-28)

More than anything her lonely adolescent life becomes a life of books, passionately pursued:

> But, after I had read for memory,
> I read for hope. The path my father's foot
> Had trod me out ... alone I carried on, and set
> My child-heart 'gainst the thorny underwood,
> To reach the grassy shelter of the trees.
> Ah babe i' the wood, without a brother-babe!
>   (I, 729-36)

She describes the moment of epiphany, when the vision dawns, and she realises her own vocation as a poet:

> Then, something moved me. Then I wakened up
> More slowly than I verily write now,
> But wholly, at last, I wakened, opened wide
> The window and my soul, and let the airs
> And outdoor sights sweep gradual gospels in,
> Regenerating what I was.
>   (I, 661-6)

and she records how she stumbles on her destiny:

>   ... Books, books, books!
> I had found the secret of a garret-room
> Piled high, packed large ...
> My books! At last, because the time was ripe,
> I chanced upon the poets.

> As the earth
> Plunges in fury, when the internal fires
> Have reached and pricked her heart ...
> ... — thus, my soul,
> At poetry's divine first finger touch,
> Let go conventions and sprang up surprised,
> Convicted of the great eternities
> Before two worlds.
> (I, 833-54)

Aurora never looks back, touched by the 'influent odours' of the Olympians and exulting,

> ... O life, O poetry,
> Which means life in life! cognisant of life
> Beyond these senses! — poetry, my life,
> My eagle, with both grappling feet still hot
> From Zeus's thunder, who has ravished me ...
> (I, 915-20)

The normal social conventions of courtship and marriage, and the patterns of the country gentry, pass her by, and on her twentieth birthday — 'Woman and artist — either incomplete' — she crowns herself solemnly with ivy in recognition that she has chosen her lonely path.

It is all very reminiscent, in tone if not in every detail, of the life of the young Elizabeth Barrett growing up in her country house on the borders of Wales, honoured by her family as the Poet Laureate of Hope End. Though she had every encouragement at home in her pursuit of her vocation, she was not excused the 'accomplishments' at which Aurora felt such frustration ('I hate needlework and drawing because I never feel occupied while I work or draw ... Dancing I consider mere idleness — I abhor music [*Autobiographical Essays*, 347-8]). Like Aurora she learned her 'complement of classic French...

> And German also ...
> [She] learnt a little algebra, a little
> Of mathematics, — brushed with extreme flounce
> The circle of the sciences.
> (I, 399-405)

but found like Aurora that 'Literature was the star which in prospect illuminated my future days: it was the spur which prompted me ... the aim ... the very soul of my being' (*Autobiographical Essays*, 351). Like Aurora, poetry comes into her life, 'Regenerating what I was'. Like Aurora again, her father is her idol, and all the literary tastes of her childhood are those he has formed.

At the same time her tastes, her ambitions and her literary activities as she passed through adolescence, are areas she shared with nobody. Though her parents applauded, and the family came to take her genius as a matter of course, she too was a 'babe i' the wood, without a brother babe'. There was nobody at Hope End with whom she could share her experience, and as much as Aurora she found herself 'Very oft alone' (I, 1092). In *Aurora Leigh* Elizabeth Barrett describes the solitary walks she makes in Hope End and the surrounding countryside as Aurora speaks of

>   ... such an up and down
> Of verdure, — nothing too much up or down,
> A ripple of land; such little hills, the sky
> Can stoop so tenderly and the wheatfields climb;
> Touch nooks of valleys lined with orchises,
> Fed full of noises by invisible streams.
>   (I, 1081-7)

and calls on Romney to admire

> The tangled hedgerows, where the cows push out
> Impatient horns and tolerant churning mouths
> 'Twixt dripping ash-boughs ...
> Hills, vales, woods, netted in a silver mist,
> Farms, granges, doubled up among the hills ...
>   (I, 1123-30)

Even the chilling figure of the aunt ('straight and calm,/Her somewhat narrow forehead braided tight ... brown hair pricked with grey/By frigid use of life') who controls Aurora's life has its parallel at Hope End. With the death of Mary Barrett in 1828 came the lengthy residence of her unmarried sister 'Bummy', who, if she was no pantomime version of a stepmother figure, still surveyed her precocious niece more levelly than did the closer family:

> My father's sister [said Aurora] started when she caught
> My soul agaze in my eyes. She could not say

> I had no business with a sort of soul,
> But plainly she objected ...
>   (I, 1030-33)

It was Bummy, it seems, who reproached her for what she perceived as slovenliness when Elizabeth appeared with a hole in her stocking, or a lack of decorum when she stayed too long with Mr Boyd, or want of observance in social form when she demurred at a boring visit to Eastnor Castle. Aurora fared worse:

>   'Would she hear my task,
> And verify my abstract of the book?
> Or should I sit down to the crochet work?
> Was such her pleasure?' Then I sat and teased
> The patient needle till it split the thread,
> Which oozed off from it in meandering lace
> From hour to hour.
>   (I, 1046-52)

but for them both

> ... through forced work and spontaneous work,
> The inner life informed the outer life.
>   (I, 1057-8)

There is no suggestion in Elizabeth's diary or her letters that Bummy, any more than Aurora's aunt, had any real interest in the poetry which was 'the very soul of my being' (*Autobiographical Essays*, 351) or identified herself at all with the passionate concerns of the young woman who found companionship only in 'the sweet familiar nature' around Hope End,

>   A nature tamed
> And grown domestic like a barn-door fowl,
> Which does not awe you with its claws and beak,
> Nor tempt you to an eerie too high up
>   (I, 634-7)

the countryside of Herefordshire.

Three:
Health — 'It Is An Endless Theme!'

Her famous ill-health, in which her father was her jealous nurse, and fiercely protected her from intrusions and demands, belongs to a period later than the Herefordshire years. The account of her early life near Ledbury — in letters, her diary, the autobiographical essays — seems to call in question the whole myth of Elizabeth Barrett's 'invalidism' from which, according to the received version, she was rescued in middle age by Robert Browning. The pictures of the young girl galloping on pony-back with such happy and healthy abandon, the camps she organized in the remoter parts of the estate at Hope End, the romping in the hay with Bro and Sam, her breathless scramblings up the Wyche for a 'chance' encounter with Boyd, and her long walks in the hills, all seem to contradict the Wimpole Street myth of later years. Nor was Elizabeth Barrett's own youthful view of herself in this mould. 'Beth', as well as being a poet, also had ambitions to be a warrior:

> When she was fifteen she would arm herself in complete steel (Beth always thought of a suit of armour and never of a red coat) and ride on a steed, along the banks of the Danube, every where by her chanted songs ... for she was to sing her own poetry all the way she went ... attracting to her side many warriors — so that by the time she reached Stamboul, Beth would be the chief of a battalion and she would destroy the Turkish empire, and deliver 'Greece the Glorious' ...
> (*Autobiographical Essays*, 361)

All her associations with her young life are of energy and vitality. Yet it does seem that her reputation for invalidism really dates from a mysterious and ultimately undiagnosed illness that attacked her (and Henrietta and Arabel) when she was fifteen. Arabel and Henrietta quickly recovered, Elizabeth did not.

It can surely be no coincidence that this period should be the one which marked the end of childhood, when Bro, her lifelong companion, departed for Charterhouse, leaving his sister at home to the mercies of Mrs Orme. Adolescence for Bro was an exciting new chapter, for his sister the dismaying end of equality with her brother, the beginning of nothing. Her reaction is a familiar one. 'Beth', as well as being a poet and a warrior, had also proposed 'to be very much in love when she was fifteen' (*Autobiographical Essays*, 361), and with a poet (probably Lord Byron). As it was, Elizabeth spent most of her fifteenth year in Gloucester under the care of doctors, much of the time in an elevated crib with suspected disease of the spine.

She returned — the ailment still undiagnosed — to convalesce at Hope End with her worried family. Writing sharply in reply to her mother's guarded suggestion that she could get better if only she tried, she had protested:

> When my dearest Mama I promised to exert myself I spoke sincerely and the promise I made I intend to keep. If it were possible, believe me, that any mental exertion could shake off bodily torture it should be effected without reluctance as without hesitation. I have exerted all my energy, all my locomotive intellects, all the muscular power of mind, and I have found that in some degree bodily anguish may be repressed from appearing, yet it has failed to be overcome.
> (*The Brownings' Correspondence*, I, 127-8)

Whatever the actual nature of the disease, we have to suppose that it was both genuine and serious, giving rise to grave apprehensions. It certainly marked the beginning of Elizabeth Barrett's lifelong concern with her health. It also gave her an excellent, if rarely acknowledged, justification for her reluctance to take part in the obligations of Victorian women in the upper-middle classes: she appears to have had no household responsibilities, even after her mother's death, other than to teach the little boys Latin. Her mother's sister 'Bummy' lived with the Barretts for long periods of time, especially after Mary Barrett's death in 1828. She was there for much of 1831-2 and 1838-41, and assumed the mother's role. Most of the regular social obligations of visiting and entertaining, which she hated, were delegated to the willing Henrietta.

Elizabeth Barrett seems to have accepted the authority of her aunt, and above that, that of her father, without demur all the time they were at Hope End and thereafter, though she was a woman of twenty-six when they left, with a growing national reputation. Her views and her opinion might have been thought worthy to consult in matters which affected the household, but there was never any suggestion that her position there was much different from Sette's and Occy's. So the smallest details of her daily life depended on her father's approval and permission, or on Bummy's leave. Requests to make use of the 'wheelbarrow' (the family vehicle), or the time-tabling of her daily life by reference to family meals, even the compulsoriness of churchgoing, were all questions settled on the whim of those she accepted as in authority over her. Tensions sometimes arose, as is clear from her diary and elsewhere, but it seems they were more obvious to her than to anybody else, and there was never any overt challenge. It was all, without doubt, the price of her 'invalidism'.

With no defined domestic position, Elizabeth was free to spend her infinite leisure, if she chose, in her room at the top of Hope End, reading, writing and thinking, and taking care of her health. There she might lie for long periods on her sofa, and read the regular parcels of books which arrived from Eaton's the booksellers: biography, travel, theology, periodicals, new novels from London, Paris and America; and poetry. She might keep up her correspondence with Bro and Hugh Boyd and a growing number of others who wrote to her as her fame spread. She might read the Greek poets in readiness for her next meeting with Boyd, or work on her translations of Aeschylus. Most importantly, she might write poetry. Not that she was housebound, or even roombound, by her health, if she chose to go out. We know of excursions she made in the country with brothers and sisters, of the regularity of her churchgoing, and of the daily household prayers which her father held and from which she never wished to be excused; and from early 1827 of her constant visits to Hugh Boyd in Great Malvern. And travel — even foreign travel — properly sanctioned and supervised by her father, was not thought beyond her. Soon after her return from Gloucester in 1823 she was sent with Henrietta for a six-month stay in Boulogne to perfect her French; and she spent months after this in Cheltenham and Hastings with relatives from both sides of the family. It does not appear, in fact, that her life was an unduly restricted one, but from fifteen her health had become a topic of concern in the family. 'Ba' had to look after herself.

Her next period of serious ill-health was in her early thirties, and was quite different from her earlier illness. It looks as though it was a form of tuberculosis, and has been diagnosed as the beginnings of the disease which finally killed her. It was a chronic lung affliction which appeared in an acute form at this period in her life, was dormant for one reason or another for twenty years, and then flared fatally when she was fifty-three.

If her mother had felt that her first illness might have an element of the psychosomatic about it, how much more could the second period of ill-health have seemed related to circumstances. In one sense her early thirties were an exhilarating time, when she was poised on the threshold of success as a writer, and recognised and acknowledged as a poet of stature. Her reputation had been advanced with the volume she published in 1838, *The Seraphim*, the first to appear under her own name, and which the press received gratifyingly. But at the same time, the last years of the decade were a time of worrying ill-health for Elizabeth. The family had finally left Hope End in 1832 for a temporary home in Sidmouth, where her health had improved considerably; but they left Devon at the end of 1835 for another temporary address, this time in Gloucester Place, Marylebone, while her father found a permanent residence in London. Here her chest fell prey to the rigours of the urban climate and the indoor life, so different from the outdoor life she had been leading in the mild environment of the south coast.

The change to the last, permanent address, only a few blocks from Gloucester Place, did little to improve Elizabeth's long-term prospects for health. With the rapid increase in population as the countryside was abandoned for the city, London was developing with dizzying speed to be the central capital of the world, and the address Edward Barrett finally settled on in Wimpole Street was one of the many new residential developments mushrooming in areas like Marylebone. But for someone of even delicate health, it was hardly an ideal locale.

Elizabeth was ill throughout the winter of 1837-1838, and recovered little health in the summer. The doctor diagnosed ulceration of the lungs which, though less dreaded than the deadly TB, was sufficiently alarming, and he ordered her to spend the following winter in a warmer climate. Edward Barrett with misgiving agreed that she should take up residence in Torquay, and, accompanied by Bro, Henrietta, and George, she left home in late August 1838 for a reluctant exile that lasted three years, and was to prove a tragic interlude in her life.

Her beloved uncle, Edward Barrett's young brother Sam, who had resigned his parliamentary seat in Richmond, Yorkshire, to administer the estates in Jamaica, died of yellow fever in 1837. That he left his favourite niece a handsome legacy and some financial independence was of small comfort. Then her brother Sam, sent out to assist his uncle in Jamaica in the aftermath of Abolition, succumbed to the same yellow fever in February 1840, the first break (apart from the infant Mary long before) in the Barrett family. Sam's death was particularly poignant, and his sister reeled under the blow. But in the summer of that year she sustained the most devastating shock of her life, of which she could almost never bring herself to speak as long as she lived.

Bro had remained with her throughout her interminable banishment, beguiling her tedium as best he could. The eldest son of the family, Bro still had no definite career to follow; he had spent some time in Jamaica between 1833 and 1835, but since his return had settled to nothing, and was a most welcome companion in Elizabeth's prolonged exile. But one day in July 1840 he left the house to sail with friends on Babbacombe Bay, and never returned. The capsized boat and his body were washed up in the bay in the early days of August.

Elizabeth lay in a state of stunned incomprehension for weeks that turned to months, bound, as she told her friend Mary Mitford in the first letter she could pen, 'in chains heavy and cold enough to be iron — and which have indeed entered into the soul' (LM, Autumn 1840). Her own health seemed irrelevant to her — her distraught father, as concerned about her as about himself, spent weeks at her side as she, whose attachment to Bro was 'literally devoted', strove to accept the death of 'the partner of my pleasures of my literary toils'. 'If to save him from anxiety ... any any effort of mine could suffice', she had declared, 'Heaven knows my heart that I would unhesitatingly buy his happiness with my own misery!' (*Autobiographical Essays*, 354). But Heaven exacted the misery without the repayment of happiness to anybody as Elizabeth lay in a coma of grief throughout the autumn.

Miss Mitford's response to Elizabeth's grief was prompt and

practical. She persuaded her friend to accept the spaniel puppy which quickly entered the Browning mythology as Flush. From the last days of 1840 every letter from Torquay carried rapturous news of Flush's exploits and progress, and the account of her final return to Wimpole Street in August 1841 is expressed in terms of Flush's experience.

Miss Mitford had selected the ideal route to Elizabeth's bruised heart. Pets had been part of her childhood at Hope End, from the squirrel which amused the little boys at their Latin lessons in her room, and the doves she kept, and the tame rabbits in the garden, to Moses the pony; and Flush was to become, according to her father, the one she loved 'better than anyone else in the world' (L, 1, 4 February 1842).

His importance to her added to the elements of the myth that now grew around her. All the elements, in fact, were now in place: her health was little better, and she had come to accept ill-health as a way of life. She rarely left the house in Wimpole Street, and was morbidly shy. She refused to make new acquaintances, and discouraged visitors to the point of refusing their advances with lies. The only personal relationships she could endure outside her family were epistolary, and these, with R.H. Horne and Benjamin Haydon, for example, flourished at a safe distance. She wore mourning throughout the year (velvet in winter, silk in summer), her notorious dependence on opium grew, and she thought of ordinary life as at an end. Poetry, always the central preoccupation of her life, now became her only motive for living. 'All my earthly futurity as an individual lies in poetry', she wrote. 'If it were not for this poetry which I feel within as a destiny to be worked out, I think I should wish to die tomorrow.'

Work she saw as one diversion for her listlessness, and established a routine. The poetry — some of the best she wrote — was to emerge as *Poems* (1844), which established her as among the leading poets of the time. The public came to know her too as a profound and learned writer on the poetry of others. At the request of the *Athenaeum* she seized the chance to deflect her despair with different work, and in 1842 she wrote a series of papers on the Greek poets of the early Christian centuries. She followed them with *The Book of the Poets*, a survey of English poetry from the Middle Ages and the Elizabethans to the Augustan poets who had formed her own taste. It ended with the triumph of the Romantics and the poetry of

Wordsworth, the king of poets: 'Vivat rex! ... We recognise the master's voice' (*The Book of the Poets*).

But Wordsworth is an old man, and the succession is open. Who will succeed him? Others, she declares in a prophetic burst, will carry poetry through what critics see as the present doldrums of poetic achievement: 'The Tennysons, the Brownings ... will work, wait on'. They will proudly embrace 'the loss of the popular cheer, of the critical assent, and of the "money in the purse"', as Wordsworth did.

The scenario is set, in fact, for the next episode in the life of Elizabeth Barrett, her meeting with Robert Browning. One of the central poems in her 1844 volume, 'Lady Geraldine's Courtship', spoke of modern poetry — Wordsworth's 'solemn-thoughted idyll, Tennyson's 'enchanted reverie', and Browning's 'Pomegranate', 'which if cut deep down the middle, / Shows a heart within deep-tinctured, of a veined humanity'. Robert Browning's attention was drawn to both, the correspondence between them started in January 1845, and the meeting followed in May. It was the beginning of a courtship and a marriage that fulfilled all the requirements of the myth. Elizabeth Barrett's health responded to the suns of Italy, and gave her fifteen years of happy married life. Indeed, recollecting her later, Thackeray's daughter noted:

> Mrs Browning was a great writer; but I think she was even more a wife and a mother than a writer, and any account of her would be incomplete which did not put these facts first and foremost in her history.
> (Guerin, *Anne Thackeray Ritchie*, 200)

Elizabeth would have been reluctant to demur.

Four:
The Upstairs Room at Hope End:
'The Growth of a Poet's Mind'

Elizabeth Barrett wasted no time during the enforced periods of inactivity which dogged her after adolescence. She had by now confirmed the seriousness of her claim to be an author by the publication of *The Battle of Marathon* (1820) and the appearance of her first poems in *The New Monthly Magazine* in 1821, and happily endorsed medical opinion that she required rest and seclusion, and prepared to make a full-time career in authorship.

Her room at the top of Hope End was her sanctum, her life there 'a retirement scarcely broken to me, except by my books and my own thoughts' (LRH, 5 October 1843). She taught the little boys Latin there, but with Bro's departure for Charterhouse in the spring of 1820, the shared lessons in Greek with his tutor Mr McSwiney had come to an end, and her education was in her own hands.

We know something of the way she spent her days in her sanctum from the little notebook she kept from 1824 to 1826, between the ages of eighteen and twenty. It has never been published, but from the notes she kept in her tiny spidery writing and the annotated lists of the books she was devouring in the upstairs room, we know all about her reading, her literary plans, and the crucial influences at work upon her between the ages of eighteen and twenty. She had already published *The Battle of Marathon* and poems in journals, and was hard at work on the *Essay on Mind*, and signposts of the works yet to come recur throughout the pages of the notebook. It is a priceless record of the growth of a poet's mind.

We know from her own account in *Glimpses Into My Own Life and Literary Character*, written when she was about fourteen, with what formidable seriousness she took the task of preparing herself to be an author: 'At SEVEN I began to think of "forming my taste"... I considered it time to see what was best to write about and read about'.

> At 7 I read the History of England and Rome — at 8 I perused the History of Greece ... Pope's *Iliad*, some parts of the *Odyssey*, passages from *Paradise Lost* selected by my dearest Mama, and some of Shakespeare's plays, among which were *The Tempest*, *Othello*, and a few historical dramatic pieces constituted my studies ... At eleven I wished to be considered an authoress ... Poetry and Essays were my studies and I felt the most ardent desire to understand the learned languages ... At twelve I enjoyed a literary life in all its pleasures.
> (*Autobiographical Essays*, 350)

As much part of her education in these impressionable years was her insatiable appetite for novels. 'My love of fiction began with my breath, and will end with it; and goes on increasing', she wrote to R. H. Horne in 1845. And so, 'Novels were still my most delightful study', she declared at ten. 'Nothing could contribute so much to my amusement as a novel. [I wished] to divert myself and to afford more scope to my nightly meditations' (*Autobiographical Essays*, 350). And from her correspondence and her notebook we know that in every spare moment she was devouring Maria Edgeworth and Sir Walter Scott, and all the new novels as they appeared.

All the new titles came to Hope End from London, and Elizabeth Barrett lists with enthusiasm all the volumes which arrived in Ledbury between 1822 and 1824. We know from her notebook that she had been reading Fanny Burney, Clara Reeve, Mary Shelley, Aphra Behn, Madame de la Fayette and, most significant of all in the formation of her impressionable mind, Madame de Stael's famous novel *Corinne*. All the reading of her formative years is to leave its mark on her writing (she had said herself at fourteen 'I read that I might write'), and none more than *Corinne*.

Corinne became a passion with her, as with so many eager young women. As early as 1832 she wrote to her friend Hugh Boyd, 'I'll have read *Corinne* for the third time, and admired it more than ever. It is an immortal book' (LB, 176). It was a book which fired ambitious, gifted women all over Europe and America who sought fame outside the family circle with a wild desire for an existence of lively independence as they fantasised about the *Corinne* lifestyle. Elizabeth Barrett read it over and over in Herefordshire, George Eliot devoured it in the Midlands, George Sand read it in France, Fanny Kemble in London, and Mary Godwin on her travels; and Harriet Beecher and Margaret Fuller and many others brooded over it in America.

The plot of *Corinne* is ridiculous. It concerns the life of a woman of genius — she dances, she sings, she paints, she acts, she writes — and her doomed love for the Scottish nobleman, Oswald, Lord Nevil. The intention of the author to demonstrate the genius of woman and her ultimate triumph is much more important; and the triumph here is not in securing the men she loves (she fails to do so), but in the public acclaim of her art. A whole generation of aspiring women rose to the message as to a trumpet call: art comes before love. Corinne (we never know her real name) is born in Italy of an English father and Italian mother. Her mother dies when she is small, but to complete her education she remains in Italy with her aunt while her father returns to England and remarries. At fifteen she rejoins him and is brought up in the bleak isolation of a small Northumberland town, where her stepmother adjures her to 'endeavour to forget all that belongs to Italy — it is to be wished that you had never known such a country'. So under the tutelage of her stepmother Lady Egramond, all her talents for music and literature are ignored and her spontaneity crushed and despised, for the society in which she finds herself endorses the provincial values of suburbia. After a particularly dismaying social evening with the local ladies, where bizarre English custom requires her decorous withdrawal before the port, Corinne declares 'The convents I had seen in Italy appeared all life to this'; and the most popular translator of the novel adds in a brisk footnote, 'What a flattering picture of female society, at the country house of an intelligent English peer!'.

But Corinne believes herself 'intended for a different career'. Italy is her salvation. When she comes of age and assumes control of her inheritance, she returns to Italy alone. When the novel opens the five years she has spent there in the development of her genius have resulted in a remarkable transformation: she is now a woman of genius, independent, uninhibited by convention, recognised and applauded by society for her achievements in writing, in acting, in music, in improvisation, living unconstrained by partner or family, wholly in charge of her own life. We see her crowned in the Capitol, in an act of public recognition, as 'the most celebrated female in Italy ...: Corinne the poet and improvisatrice, one of the loveliest women of Rome'. She is the Genius of Women, an amalgam of all that woman is capable of (though she wants only to be 'judged as a poet as an artist') and it is only in Italy that she can thrive.

As seen through the eyes of Corinne, Italy assumes almost mythic proportions, and magical properties. It is the golden land of promise where everything is possible, a smiling land of warmth, the cradle of the arts, the centre of vitality and spontaneity, the contradiction of all the barbarisms of 'Northumberland'. England, in *Corinne*, and especially the mysterious north of England, represents the stifling of all creative urges in women, and the inhibition of natural impulse.

Elizabeth Barrett, with a legion of other gifted and frustrated young women, eagerly absorbed the myth of Italy created by Madame de Stael, as she pored over the novel in her upstairs room at Hope End and identified with Corinne. The books that came from London added regularly to the library of books on Italy and *Corinne* which she seemed to be accumulating, and which were to have, of course, so significant an effect on her own later life when she secretly left her father's house as a married woman and chose a new home in Florence. At twenty she was quite enthralled with the novel, and by the time she was twenty-four she records in a letter that she had read it three times. A year later she is declaring, '[It] deserves to be read three score and ten times — that is, once every year in the age of man' (LB, 176). Many other details confirm the effect *Corinne* was having on her impressionable young mind. Among the books in 'the *Corinne* Industry' which arrived at Hope End and were meticulously recorded in her notebook is a volume by the poetess Letitia Landon, who published as L.E.L., which she speaks of warmly. She was certainly familiar with L.E.L.'s work, because Miss Landon had put into English the Odes in *Corinne*, in the most popular translation of the novel; and L.E.L.'s own long poem *The Improvisatrice* was inspired by *Corinne*, herself the Improvisatrice. Elizabeth Barrett greeted the volume warmly, though with caution.

She was a discriminating critic of contemporary literature who had spent all her youth sedulously forming her taste, and by twenty was quite confident about what was good and what was bad. L.E.L., a young woman from another good Herefordshire family and another disciple of Madame de Stael, had already published copiously, and her work had previously failed to provoke much enthusiasm from the lofty Elizabeth Barrett. She had found L.E.L., her notebook tells us, 'weak', and wholly lacking in 'the warmth and colouring, the masterdom of outline, the elegance of style', which characterise great poetry. What revitalised Elizabeth Barrett's view of L.E.L. is, perhaps predictably, *The Improvisatrice*. She had read the rather dismissive notice in the *Westminster Review*, where L.E.L. is checked for her 'puny and sickly thoughts', and responded with some indignation. In her own notes on *The Improvisatrice* and *The Troubadour* the severe young critic rises from her previous dismissal of L.E.L.'s poetry as *'dull* — the dullest things I ever read' to an acknowledgement that her work on *Corinne* is 'beautiful and graceful, showing great intensity of feeling and vivacity of imagination'. Her enthusiasm however, even in this context, is still guarded. She adds, 'At *present* I am far from considering Miss Landon superior or even equal to Mrs Hemans in practical execution', though later she reversed this opinion. She has not recorded in the notebook what in Felicia Hemans's poetry she found so far in advance of L.E.L.'s, but in mood and sympathy and their enthusiasm for Madame de Stael they all meet on common ground. Mrs Hemans declared to a friend that *Corinne* had a power over her which was quite indescribable; 'some passages seem to give me back my own thoughts and feelings, my whole inner being', and had marked such a passage in her own copy, and written against it, 'C'est moi'.

There were other authors in Elizabeth Barrett's collection who witness to the cult of *Corinne*. One who spoke like Mrs Hemans of the effects of the novel was Anna Jameson, author of *Diary of an Ennuyée*; we know from the notebook that Elizabeth Barrett was reading that book as it came out in 1824. *The Diary of an Ennuyée* was notable in its day as what has been called 'one of the most charming English imitations of *Corinne*' (Ellen Moers, *Literary Women*, 1975, 188), and presents an English version of the heroine in the mortally sick young poetess whose account we read. Elizabeth Barrett's encounter with the book is the more interesting in the light of her subsequent warm friendship with Anna Jameson when Elizabeth was in Italy. But in these earlier days she knew Mrs Jameson only as the author of the engaging narrative which, in the guise of a traveller's diary, outlined the enthusiasms, experiences, anecdotes and reflections of the young invalid as she made her leisurely way round all the sights of Italy. As in *Corinne*, the stages of the journeys between Venice, Florence, Rome, Naples, and all the monuments of the cities, and even the eruption of Vesuvius, are listed together with the musings to which they give rise. 'O, what a country is this'! ... 'All that I see I *feel* — all that I *feel* sinks so deep into my heart and into my memory' ... 'And to find my own feelings reflected from the pages of a book [*Corinne*] in language too deeply and eloquently true', sighs the stricken diarist (*Diary of an Ennuyée*, 116).

Throughout the narrative we learn that *Corinne* is 'the fashionable *vade mecum* for [all] sentimental travellers in Italy' (*Diary of an Ennuyée*, 115) and the first visit as the travellers pass through France is to the chateau of Madame de Stael at Le Coppet.

* * *

Though Elizabeth Barrett had not, at this stage, been to Italy, she had done the next best thing in vicariously profiting from the experience of others. She had even tried to battle, she tells us, through the three volumes of *The English in Italy* (the third volume, she considered in her notebook, defeated her — 'and I thought very highly of my good temper in getting so far'!). It is a very long, tedious collection of stories ('one hardly knows whether the last yawn or the last chapter should be thought of first') in which the author attempted to characterise the English abroad, specifically in Italy, by fictionalised accounts of the types to be met in Naples, Genoa, Rome and so on. The narratives demonstrate the national characteristics of such representative individuals as 'L'Amoroso', 'Il Politico', 'Il Zingari', and 'Il Critico'. Elizabeth Barrett had abandoned the book guiltily for something lighter, she admits. Hogg's *Winter Evening Tales* had been waiting for her for some time, and she enjoyed his fiction as much as his poetry. Perhaps it was a time of illness? While it is reassuring for the easy-going reader of today to find the precocious young blue-stocking of Hope End flagging, it is puzzling to see why it should have been Lord Normanby's pretentious character studies in *The English in Italy* which defeated her. She was, after all, simultaneously coping with eight volumes of Madame de Genlis' *Memoirs* without demur.

More profitable reading than the *Tales* perhaps was Alaric Watts' new *Literary Souvenir* which appeared for the first time in 1825. It was an annual anthology of the year's popular literature, and regularly contained poems by Mrs Hemans, L.E.L. and other poetesses, plus stories and engravings, and, almost a recurrent motif, tales and accounts of Italy: 'The Bay of Naples', 'Imilda de Lanbetazzi: An Italian Tale', and 'Rosamunda: A Venetian Fragment' all appeared in the first two numbers which the notebook shows Elizabeth to have read.

Italy, and the myth of *Corinne*, were a solid part of her literary background. In her own work it all shows most obviously perhaps in her later masterpiece, her 'novel in verse' *Aurora Leigh*, which reads sometimes like a versification of *Corinne*. But in fact, though it overlaps in innumerable ways with Madame de Stael, *Aurora Leigh* debates the questions and modifies the conclusions of *Corinne*.

Madame de Stael was no novelist, and the plot and its handling in *Aurora Leigh* show Elizabeth Barrett with the same shortcomings in 'practical execution' that she attributed to Mrs Hemans' poetry. But with Madame de Stael it is the ideas which electrify, rather than the practical execution; ideas and questions which Elizabeth Barrett has eagerly absorbed and which find expression in the poetry of *Aurora Leigh*.

Primarily, of course, the theme of *Corinne* and *Aurora Leigh* are the same, the growth and development of the woman as artist, and in both the necessary ground for this is Italy. Both Corinne and Aurora Leigh spend their formative years in Italy, their mothers' home, but are obliged to pass their adolescence elsewhere, for Aurora Leigh's father is an austere Englishman and Corinne's is an English peer. All that they encounter in their fathers' homeland is the bleak contradiction of the ideology of the south, for one returns to the harshness of her stepmother and the other to a narrow-minded maiden aunt who has lived 'A sort of cage bird life, born in a cage' (I, 305).

Marriage and love, and the alternatives to them, are the themes that inform both texts: society, in the form of her aunt, pressurises Aurora to marry her cousin Romney, the social theorist, while Corinne endures the anguish of forbidden love for Oswald. Both, it seems, must make the choice between art and the lot of 'a common woman'. Aurora has quite other plans than those formulated for her by her aunt, and refuses marriage with Romney because, as she says,

> ... What you love
> Is not a woman, Romney, but a cause;
> You want a helpmate, not a mistress, Sir, ...
> You have a wife already whom you love,
> Your social theory.
>   (II, 400-10)

and as she points out:

> I too have my vocation, — work to do ...
> 'I am born', I said with firmness, 'I,'
> To walk another way than his ...
> (II, 455, 580-1)

On her twentieth birthday she stood consciously on the threshold of life, 'Woman and artist, — either incomplete. Both credulous of completion' — and solemnly crowned herself, witnessed by the unseen Romney, with an ivy wreath in anticipation of her noblest ends. Romney's subsequent urgent plan — that she join in his quest to save the world — she steadfastly puts by in the name of the superior claims of art. It is poets who will save the world. They are

> ... the only truth tellers now left to God,
> The only speakers of essential truth,
> The only teachers who instruct mankind.
> (I, 859-865)

She pursues her vocation and embraces her destiny; her poetry creates the conditions from which Romney can create his new social order. His mission has been 'to rescue men /By half-means, half-way, seeing half their wants,' a political scheme which only poetry can complete.

The sensational plot of the 'verse-novel' in which the theme is set looks back to *Corinne*. Aurora's mother dies, and after her father's death when she is thirteen she is sent back to England to the mercies of an unsympathetic aunt. The aunt has no understanding of Aurora's yearnings — she

> ... demurred
> That souls were dangerous things to carry straight
> Through all the spilt saltpetre of the world.
> (I, 1033-1035)

and attempts to make her niece into her idea of a womanly woman.

From this prison Aurora plans her mission as a woman of genius. Refusing marriage and social concern with Romney, she begins to make her mark as a poet:

> [I] bade him mark that, howsoe'er the world

Went ill, as he related, certainly
The thrushes still sung in it.
    (I, 1113-5)

Romney, in total consistency with his cause of social equality, decides to marry the factory girl, Marian Erle, but is thwarted again — his intended bride is tricked, smuggled to France, and raped. Aurora, finding her in Paris, rescues her and settles with her and her child in Italy, the golden land, where she plans her masterpiece. Romney goes to them in Italy. He had established the ideal community in his own mansion, but it was destroyed by fire, and Romney blinded (by Marian's father as it chances).

In the discussion and resolution of all the misunderstandings of the past, Aurora proposes that

We both were wrong that June-day ...
            I who talked of art,
And you who grieved for all men's griefs ...
    (VIII, 552-4)

After all, 'Art is much but Love is more' (IX, 656), and she agrees to become his wife. Here Barrett and de Stael part company, of course. While Aurora and Romney arrive at a sublime compromise of ideals, represented in their marriage ('Art symbolises heaven, but Love is God /And makes heaven' [IX, 657-8]), Corinne is balked of her desire when Oswald, Lord Nevil, her ideal, follows his father's wishes and chooses her half-sister, Lucy. Corinne forfeits love for ambition and sacrifices marriage for art. It was a clash of principle which Elizabeth Barrett herself was to experience not long afterwards when she made the choice between Edward Barrett and filial obligation, and Robert Browning and love.

The obsession with Italy and the implications of all that it offered mark much of the reading Elizabeth Barrett was doing as she prepared herself for her vocation; but not all her novel reading reflected it. Other novels suggest other forces at work, and illuminate other questions which perplex a young writer. She was scarcely twenty, and although she had published precociously she had still to establish her own identity as a writer. All her juvenilia, ambitious though it was (her epic, *The Battle of Marathon*, had already appeared, and she was writing her *Essay on Mind*), was perforce heavily derivative, and she was conscious that her own identity had still to be defined.

In the long hours she spent alone in the privacy of her room at Hope End, she pondered and reflected on the nature of Life and Art, and the contributions to be made by the different sexes. *Corinne* had discussed life, art, and the role of women in passionate terms, and left a powerful and permanent impression on Elizabeth Barrett; and other novels made their own mark.

Madame de Stael's *Corinne* had been directly concerned with the themes dear to Elizabeth Barrett's heart, the questions of woman and art and the potential clash between a woman's defined role and her own sense of vocation and an alternative lifestyle. Elizabeth Barrett had responded to it warmly. It is interesting that two other novels she was devouring in 1824, though different from Madame de Stael, impressed her as powerfully. One was *Matthew Wald* by Scott's biographer J.G. Lockhart, which proved as magnetically compulsive as *Corinne*. Elizabeth Barrett was swept off her feet by it. There are two pages of the notebook in her spidery writing:

> About three months ago I laid down this book with an awakened imagination and a thrilling heat ... Novels, like water colours, generally fly with time. It is very rarely that thinking of a novel three months or even three weeks after its perusal we can conjure up the passionate feeling which haunted us then. I don't know whether I dare name among these rare works the one before me, but it is certain that the deep footmarks which *MW* made in his peregrination over my mind are not yet green. A very spiritual, sensible soul hath stepped into the bodily structure of the little book, [and] hath given it, if so I might say, the expressive countenance of poetry. There is a fitful wildness and startling passion and subduing energy. I like the book ...

What is it about this novel that so impressed the young Elizabeth? It is a sensational and ultimately pessimistic work, compressed into a single short volume, about a central character searching for his identity, and so framed that it is hardly surprising that a young mind, looking eagerly for experience, even at second hand, should react so passionately to it. Against a sombre background of Calvinist thinking Matthew Wald, a well-born Scottish youth orphaned at Culloden, tries to establish how he can maintain his integrity in the face of the conflicting demands of society, but ultimately fails to find any permanent meaning in life.

Because of a quirk in his father's will, Matthew Wald is balked of his inheritance, and his father's fortune and estate go to his cousin Katherine, with whom he has always been in love. It is no conventional relationship, however, for in the terms of the novel Katherine represents the completion of himself, and as he grows up under a hostile, violent guardian Katherine is the one positive aspect of his life. She is forced into marriage with a wealthy blackguard; and Matthew, with growing cynicism, reviews the professions open to him. In turn he enters the army, the law, medicine, sets up his own business, takes a post as a private tutor, finally, by a succession of quirks in the plot, becomes a landowner, a minor aristocrat, and Member of Parliament.

The central episode of the plot is located in Matthew's period as a private tutor in the household of Sir Claud Barr. The eldest daughter of the house, the mysterious and apparently undervalued Miss Joanne, is, he learns by another twist in the plot, the illegitimate child of Sir Claud's earliest passion, a wild, beautiful Flemish woman with whom he eloped, but was forbidden to marry by all the conventions of society. Sir Claud has instead been obliged to marry the disdainful Lady Juliana. But the rejected victim appears at his wedding with their child, and commits suicide dramatically under the wheels of the wedding coach. The baby, Miss Joanne, is an embarrassing addition to the family.

Matthew Wald, touched by the story, sees it as his duty to rescue this victim of social proprieties and the sins of a previous generation, and marries her. It is a calm, dispassionate marriage of principle, about which he never allows himself to be rueful, though the thoughts rise unbidden:

> There was always a certain dark, self-reproaching thought that haunted me. A thousand and a thousand times did my lips tremble to utter 'I love you, Joanne,' but it is not *that* love...
> (*Matthew Wald*, 227)

Later in the novel he is able to prove Joanne's rightful claim on the Barr estates (Sir Claud had written to her mother 'Je vous jure, vous serrez — vous êtes — mon épouse', sufficient in Scots law to establish her daughter's right) and Matthew thus becomes — ironically — the Laird of Barrmains. With equal irony, his wife, the rightful inheritor of a noble line, turns to the people and embraces the tenets of the Calvinistic Methodists.

Meanwhile his own first love, Katherine, is unhappily married to a brutal, adulterous aristocrat. Information about his scandalous life filters through. In the end Matthew challenges him to a duel and murders him violently:

> I spitted him through the heart — I rushed on till the hilt stopped me — I did not draw my steel out of him — I spurned him off it with my foot. 'Lie there — rot there, beast!' — a single groan and his eye fixed ... I dipped my shoe in his blood.
>   (*Matthew Wald*, 359)

But Katherine dies too from shock, and Joanne, who has witnessed Matthew and Katherine in a final, more than cousinly embrace, miscarries with his child and dies as well. Matthew is confined in a madhouse. His ultimate release brings him no deliverance from the manic depression which haunts him, 'the secret slave of despondence', and he dies without ever discovering a real meaning to life. Resignation and the acceptance of a hostile universe seem the most positive lesson to be found in Lockhart's narrative.

It does not seem surprising that Elizabeth Barrett was swept off her feet by the novel, in spite of its sensationalism and implausibility as a story. (What is surprising, perhaps, is that she should have been allowed to read it at all!) It is not the narrative so much as the reflections caused by the events in the narrative that are important, for the moments of intense feeling were what left the most abiding impression on Elizabeth Barrett, and were to appear later in *Aurora Leigh*.

Themes and motifs occur and overlap continually between Elizabeth Barrett's early reading and *Aurora Leigh*. Both documents are about marriage, and the motives acknowledged, unconscious and repressed which inform choices and the results which follow them. Matthew Wald and Romney Leigh share characteristics. Their ideology in marriage is directly similar, for instance. Romney Leigh, on principle, commits himself to a loveless marriage with Marian Erle the working class girl (he does not actually marry her — she stands him up at the church door), to further his ideals for a classless society: Matthew Wald marries Joanne to correct the injustice of society's conventions. The whole issue of marriage is one that is explored in both texts, crudely perhaps in *Matthew Wald*, with more conscious sophistication in *Aurora Leigh*. But both deal with the same duality, marriage as a social duty versus marriage as a love commitment. Matthew Wald finds, too late, that he should have followed his first impulse and secured Katherine: Romney, in time, is persuaded that personal commitment can be more important than political principle, and marries Aurora.

Marriage is a question that is resolved happily (though leaving further questions unresolved) in *Aurora Leigh*, left irresolute in the less conventional *Matthew Wald*. Elizabeth Barrett, following Charlotte Bronte, shows Aurora Leigh triumphantly married to the blinded Romney, who agrees that the world will be saved by art and the inspired individual sooner than through his principles of progress organised for the people as a whole. Their marriage is a symbol of recognition that to raise men's bodies you must first raise their souls. And Aurora Leigh concedes in turn that one must work with as well as for humanity. It is certainly an advance on Lockhart's negative conclusions: there is a meaning to life, and it can be perceived.

J.G. Lockhart's material and the use made of it in *Matthew Wald* anticipate Elizabeth Barrett's in *Aurora Leigh*. Many readers in 1857 were shocked by the frank sexual references in *Aurora Leigh* to prostitution and rape. Romney Leigh's intended bride, Marian Erle, is betrayed and raped and left with an illegitimate child, and as a child Marian herself was sold to the highest bidder by her parents. So rape, prostitution, illegitimacy and childbirth are all explicit topics in Elizabeth Barrett's mature work. But they had been the topics of her surprisingly uncensored reading at Hope End when she was eighteen.

The illegitimacy of Matthew Wald's wife Joanne, has already been mentioned as a central point of that novel. But it has been anticipated immediately beforehand by the parallel story of a kindly old minister Mr Meikle, whose son, it transpires, seduced a village girl before his death of consumption, and left the old man with an unlooked-for grandson when the mother fled in shame, too afraid to face the strictures of society. The story is merely an episode in Matthew Wald's search for a meaning in life, for Mr Meikle has no further part in the novel, and has no obvious part in the structure except as a parallel with Sir Claud Barr, his mistress and his child. Elizabeth Barrett used Marian Erle and her child as evidence for Aurora Leigh's argument that personal commitment with individuals is more important than a social programme, as she demonstrates in the section where the two women live together with the child, and

Aurora Leigh completes her masterpiece. But in *Matthew Wald* the use of the theme is much more pessimistic — nothing positive seems to emerge from this flouting of the social code. Even Mr Meikle's little grandson already shows signs of his father's complaint, and will not long survive him. Elizabeth Barrett in fact identified the material, and made good use of it for her own purposes later. *Matthew Wald* is a bleak but powerful novel, and it stayed in her mind.

Elizabeth Barrett responds to the sheer energy of *Matthew Wald*, and the multiple varieties of experience, either described in the frankest terms, or implied. It has something of the characteristics of the primitive picaresque tale, the novel held together as much by the personality of the hero as by the design of the author; but where the early picaresque hero is simply a peg on which the author hangs episode, experience and anecdote, Matthew Wald is a full and developing character through whom the author presents a full and chilling world-view.

It is also a deeply Calvinistic novel, where a belief in the stern doctrines of predestination and reprobation is implicit throughout. Matthew Wald is not one of the elect, and no saving grace is available to him. His wife Joanne, in the grip of religious mania and preaching predestination and the depravity of man, is Lockhart's mocking mouth-piece. The young Elizabeth responded with a thrilling heart and a shudder, but was clearly fascinated. Her own religion was private and intense. She had been brought up in no particular church, and the family was as at home, and familiar, in all the meeting houses of the Dissenters as in the parish church. At twelve she had declared her impatience with all organised religion, though proclaiming her own sincere faith, and she wrote much later to an anxious correspondent that, while Arminians might call her a Calvinist, and Calvinists an Arminian, she felt herself that she belonged simply to the Brotherhood of all Believers, and stood for free will and responsibility. But this was the considered opinion of her maturity, twenty years after her passionate response to *Matthew Wald*. At eighteen she was eagerly open to all varieties of religious experience, even the grim doctrines of Calvinism.

Elizabeth Barrett was rather overwhelmed by *Matthew Wald*; but another new novel she was reading that year (1824) she weighs and finds wanting. This was *The Pilot*, 'by the Author of *The Spy*', in fact James Fenimore Cooper. Maybe it was a period of one of her unexplained illnesses and her health made her tetchy, because

immediately before *The Pilot* she seems to have been reading something called *Memoirs of the Ionian Islands* by a General de Vaudan-
court, and dismisses that very briskly as 'not at all an interesting
work, maugre its subject, written in a very dry, ungraceful style'. So
the next book she picks up, *The Pilot*, provokes the same critical tone.
It shows 'some fine drawing here, a free routine and a master's touch;
but our Author does not excel in delicate finishing. The last chapter
is lamentably bad'. All the same, Elizabeth Barrett was storing it
away for future use. Although the subtitle is 'A Tale of the Sea',
Elizabeth Barrett read there other more interesting themes, some of
which will be put to use in her own work later.

The Pilot is a story about the American War of Independence, about
the confrontation of an old society and a new society (as, in a sense
Aurora Leigh was to be about an old society, Romney's, and a new
society, Marian's, and the violent confrontation between them), and
how the new society is seeking to break with the old.

We know about Elizabeth Barrett's own early interest in foreign
politics — it was one of her most notable characteristics later when
she was in Italy when she was obsessed with contemporary French
and Italian politics — from her other reading at Hope End at this
time. She notes having read Colonel Stanhope's *Greece in 1823 and
1824* for instance, and William Leake's *An Historical Outline of the
Greek Revolution*. And we know that she is likely to be interested to
some extent in the War of Independence because she had just been
reading *Considerations of the French Revolution* by her admired role-
model Madame de Staël, which contains an important chapter on
the subject, 'Thoughts on the American War'. Elizabeth Barrett
called the book 'amazingly eloquent and wonderfully prejudiced'!

But another theme in *The Pilot* of enormous interest to Elizabeth
Barrett is that of women and gender-roles, and this lends more grist
to her mill. Certainly *Matthew Wald* had explored with vigour the
question of woman as social or sexual victim, and that was a theme,
as we have seen, that Elizabeth Barrett adopted for her own use in
Aurora Leigh. But *Matthew Wald*, with its male author and male
narrator, was heavily orientated toward the male viewpoint. *The
Pilot* has a different perspective. It is a yarn about espionage and
naval combat, but these patriarchal areas are significantly manipu-
lated by women, and the whole question of gender is an important
one in it. Elizabeth Barrett certainly thought it was, for she discusses
it in her notes on the novel in the notebook.

Cecilia Howard and Katherine Plowden are important characters who have different functions and different images in the novel. Elizabeth Barrett ponders them both. 'Our Author', she snorts, 'intending to convey feminine gentleness in Cecilia Howard, has made bad work of it' — and what she means by this, I think, is that the aspect of woman conveyed by 'our Author' in Cecilia Howard is a presentation that she dislikes. Cecilia Howard is what Cooper must have thought of as the archetypal image of femininity. She is demure, she is submissive (although she has a measure of independence, she is happier as a follower) and when we first meet her she is engaged, very properly, on an ambitious project of needlework and serving coffee to her uncle.

Her cousin Katherine Plowden on the other hand, Elizabeth Barrett views with warm approval — 'Her cousin', she tells us, 'I like to my soul!'. She first appears in the novel, interestingly enough, disguised as a boy, a resourceful and imaginative way to contact her lover, an intrepid American sea-captain, who is under arms and still loyal to King George. Nor is she merely a tomboy — she loses no jot of proper modesty in her male costume. Cooper, having it both ways, tell us 'Female bashfulness was beautifully contrasted to her attire'.

Katherine efficiently organises her cousin Cecilia and another woman to act in counter-espionage against the rebels; and at the conclusion of a long, long novel (a conclusion Elizabeth Barrett found 'lamentably bad — as commonplace as talking of the weather') Katherine is happily married to the dauntless Captain Barnstable. And Cooper adds that since she is childless she is able to accompany her husband on every voyage, and has been to every part of the globe with him. Probably it is not these details which Elizabeth Barrett found so commonplace, but Cooper's reversion at the end to traditional gender-roles: however independent Katherine may have proved herself throughout the narrative, at the end the author has to revert to the conventional mode. Cecilia, of course, predictably marries the pilot.

Now neither Katherine Plowden nor Cecilia Howard is obviously a model for Aurora Leigh: neither young woman is involved in the kind of artistic creativity which Elizabeth Barrett saw as the ultimate human achievement, that is, poetry. But without doubt Elizabeth Barrett is thinking about the 'Woman Question' here, so much a topic of discussion in the 1850s, and her brisk notes confirm it. The female characters are involved with a central question of feminism, the self-determination of women. What Elizabeth Barrett does not like about Cecilia Howard is her willingness to accept definition in male terms, on how she responds to a patriarchal world; and her warmth for Katherine Plowden is very much directed to her rejection of gender roles.

It is one thing, after all, that *Aurora Leigh* is about — the right of women to define themselves. Her reading of novels in the impressionable years at Hope End was as much a part of preparation for her own vocation as a poet as all her conscious study of the poets.

Elizabeth Barrett was passionately addicted to novels all her life, and a high proportion of her reading at Hope End, we learn from her notebook and later from her correspondence, was fiction; but it is interesting — and perhaps predictable — that the novel never for a moment displaced her first commitment to poetry. As she prepared herself anxiously for her vocation as a poet we know that she worked her way (certainly between the ages of eighteen and twenty, the time covered by her notebook) systematically through the works of Milton, Shakespeare, Pope and Dryden among the English poets as well as Dante, Voltaire, Boccaccio and Machiavelli. As background reading she was working at Kant, Berkeley and Spinoza, and kept records in her notebook of her progress. She also kept abreast, of course, (and she records it) with all the modes and conventions of the poetry of the day. She was, famously, to say later that she had no grandmothers to follow: England had many learned women — and yet where were the poets? There had been no continuing tradition of women poets to act as role models for aspiring female talent, and in their absence she turned, perforce, to male models.

The established poets of her formative years, and the generation before it, marked an uneasy time of transition, and she was beginning to be conscious of it. There were few obvious giants in the land in her youth, though many in waiting. Keats, Byron and Shelley were dead, Coleridge was writing nothing, Wordsworth's phenomenal outpouring of the early century had come to an end, and though he lingered on until 1850 as Poet Laureate, by 1810 his significant work was done. The admired writers of the day in the 1820s and 1830s were Harrison Ainsworth, Barry Cornwall and Mary Russell Mitford and among the poetesses Letitia Landon, Mrs Hemans and Anna Seward. For literary giants she looked back to Shenstone, Beattie, Akenside and Cowper, poets of the later eighteenth century who wrote outside the school of Pope and are often credited with representing the stirrings of the movement in poetry which emerged at the end of the century as the Romantic school.

Elizabeth Barrett read them with critical discernment. She describes her first encounter with Beattie's *The Minstrel* in an early autobiographical essay:

> The brilliant imagery, the fine metaphors, and the flowing numbers of *The Minstrel* truly astonished me. Every stanza excited my ardent admiration, nor can I now remember the delight which I felt on perusing these pages without enthusiasm.
> (*Autobiographical Essays*, 350)

She records her first meeting with the poetry of Shenstone in rather different terms. His poetry is important to her in that it becomes a touchstone by which she defined her own views on the nature of the poet. The encounter itself is a disappointing experience. ('I have heard of Shenstone ever since I heard of poetry — and now that I have read him I feel surprised how Shenstone should ever have been heard of', *Notebook*.) But her disappointment with his 'cold and inanimate versification' and lack of thought leads her to conclude that Shenstone's chosen life as a country gentleman has proved fatal to his genius ('if he had any!') — 'An unagitated life, starving of necessary nutrient, is not the life for a Poet.'

> His mind should ever and anon be transplanted like a young tree. It should be allowed to shoot its roots in a free soil, and not vegetate in a corner. Look at the lives of our great poets — Shakespeare's, Milton's, Byron's — and find the truth of this.
> (*Notebook*)

Shenstone's genius 'died of a *faim*'! It is all consistent with her views in the Preface to *The Battle of Marathon* that intellectual vigour is as necessary to poetry as 'Fancy' — and on which she is working herself ('For Poesy's whole presence, when defined, / Is elevation of the reasoning mind' [*Essay on Mind*, 944-5]).

When she was planning the Preface for her own *Essay on Mind* ('an Ethic Poem') in 1826 she was looking both backwards and forwards at the progress of poetry. The notebook contains notes and a draft for the Preface. She revised them before publication; but at this point she muses on the question of modern poetry with precocious

1. A watercolour sketch of Hope End, believed to be by Elizabeth's sister, Henrietta

2. A rare photograph of Hope End before its demolition in 1872

3. Ruby Cottage, home of Hugh Stuart Boyd

4. Oil painting of Edward, Henrietta and Elizabeth Barrett

5. George, Arabella, Samuel and Charles Barrett.
Oil painting by William Artaud

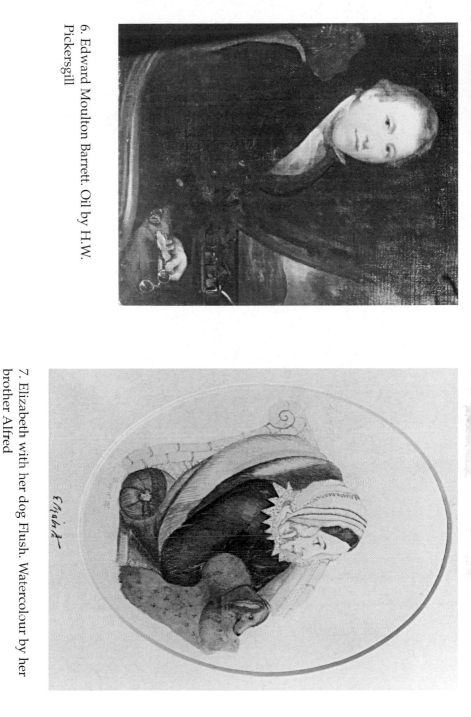

6. Edward Moulton Barrett. Oil by H.W. Pickersgill

7. Elizabeth with her dog Flush. Watercolour by her brother Alfred

8. The first page of Robert Browning's first letter to Elizabeth Barrett

9. Robert Browning, painted by D.G. Rossetti, 1855

10. Elizabeth Barrett Browning,
portrait by Michele Gordigiani, 1858

solemnity. 'The elegance of Campbell and the sportive simplicity of Rogers', she remarks,

> have cleared a happy passage for the less-distinguished aspirers to didactic learning [herself!] and have rendered that noble branch of intellect and poetry, though not the characteristic of the age, yet one of its fairest ornaments.
> (*Notebook*)

In fact, the poetry of the later eighteenth century characterised by (as she saw it) a certain superficiality and a lack of intellectual vigour, was yielding to a new deep seriousness of intent, a new perception of the essence of poetry. She views it as a seriousness of thought and conception rather than expression, however: the new profundity and solemnity of poetry is formulated with a deceptive lightness. 'Some years back the language of the public mind was serious and didactic; it is now light and imaginative' (*Notebook*). Imagination, in fact, was the key element absent from Augustan poetry, and this is how universal mystical truth is to be imparted. Her own *Essay on Mind*, she intends, should bridge the gap between 'philosophy' and 'poetry', and the reader should find that 'Poetry is not only Fancy, and Philosophy is not only learning', and that the learned and the reflective, and the aspiring and the imaginative, can indeed be united.

The *Essay on Mind* is a real attempt at her own voice in poetry, but it is not the first. In form the *Essay on Mind* is an impressive imitation of Pope; yet her first long poem, *The Battle of Marathon*, an epic account in four books of heroic couplets of the Greek victory in the fight for freedom against the Persians, embodies themes which are her own — Greece, freedom, Byron, the nature of poetry, the role of the poet. She follows directions the Romantic poets have pointed to in the topics she celebrates. Freedom in all its forms, political and personal, was to be a theme which obsessed her all her life, and through all her poetry. (Her first published poem in 1821 was 'Stanzas, Excited by Some Reflections on the Present State of Greece', and 'Lines on the Death of Lord Byron' appeared in 1824.)

Her ideas on the nature of poetry were still forming. Her first instinctive yearnings were towards the poets of her childhood:

> Cowper sang in England, and Thomas Warton also ... and Beattie, for whom we have too much love to analyse it, seeing

that we drew our childhood's first poetic pleasure from his
Minstrel! and Burns walked in glory on the Scottish mountain-
side ... It was the revival of poetry — the putting down of the
Dryden dynasty ... For Nature and Poetry did embrace one
another!
(*The Book of the Poets*)

Her idea of what made poetry, though it eagerly anticipated every
development, always included the poets who had first formed her
taste and her earliest poetry reflects it. 'Cowper's Grave', published
in 1838 but written earlier (he died in 1800) to honour a poet she
venerated, is a wholly eighteenth century poem, which conveys the
conventional message of Christian redemption and the divinity
through the atonement of human suffering. 'The Pet Name' in the
same volume is a nostalgic poem that looks back to her childhood
at Hope End and the birthday rituals there. Without mentioning the
name, she ascribes it to Bro:

> My brother gave that name to me
> When we were children twain,
> When names acquired baptismally
> Were hard to alter, as to see
> That life had any pain —
>   ('The Pet-Name', 31-35)

and thinks lovingly of her father's part:

> My father's promise I did not miss,
> When stooping down he cared to kiss
> The poet at his knee.
>   (Ibid., 48-50)

Both poems are unlike anything she was to write in her maturity,
and are a looking back to the poetry of her youth.

If we are to believe her notebook and her diary, she was as
systematic in her study of modern poetry as she had been entertained by the new novels. Hogg, 'the Ettrick Shepherd', makes the
most frequent appearance in her reading list, and Montgomery and
Shenstone follow. Her standards are high, her criticism severe, but
it is genuine critical evaluation she recorded. Moreover, she has
moved with the times in her observation, and the times have
changed. By 1822, for instance, Elizabeth Barrett has encountered

Wordsworth, and after *Lyrical Ballads* and *The Excursion*, she never read poetry in quite the same way again.

Whatever her affection for the poets who first fired her own ambitions, her apprehension of the nature and material of poetry is drawn from the Romantic poets. Intellectual rigour was what she most admired about the school that flourished in the early years of the century (and what had presumably most dismayed other more conventional readers, like her friend Mrs Martin, who was apparently quite defeated by 'The Ancient Mariner'). In these years Wordsworth stands paramount for Elizabeth Barrett, though she warmed to the 'dauntless originality and sublime conception' of Coleridge, and some of the volumes of Keats and Shelley, published not very long before she writes about them in her diary, left her breathless — 'Shelley's "Adonais" [1821]... is perfectly exquisite. Oh! it is so beautiful!' (*Diary*, 138). About Keats she is more thoughtfully detailed. The sensuous effects of 'The Eve of St. Agnes' and 'Isabella' (the elements most appealing to later Victorians) left her unmoved, but she responded enthusiastically to the 'poetry of wonderful grandeur' in 'Hyperion':

> The effect of the appearance of Hyperion, among the ruined Titans, is surprisingly fine. Poor poor Keats ... Like his own Saturn, he was dethroned from the seat which his genius claimed: and in the radiance of his own Hyperion will he appear to posterity ...
> (*Diary*, 93)

Keats was 'a true poet, from his first works to his last', a poet of 'endurant construction'. But Wordsworth, all the same, as she insisted to Boyd, is 'the greater poet ... the profounder thinker, the nearer to the poetic secrets of nature, more universal, more elevated' (LB, 254).

She encountered Wordsworth early on, and throughout her life it was he who represented for her the fullest definition of what poetry was. All her correspondence is full of her veneration for him, beginning with her earliest letters to Mr Boyd, who is reproached more than once for his failure to share her enthusiasm; and when her cousin, John Kenyon, who knew everybody, invited her to meet the poet in 1836, it was her proudest day.

Wordsworth is the poet from whom she learned most. One significant way in which the Romantics changed English poetry was in their description and presentation of the relation between man and nature, and Elizabeth Barrett absorbed this and modified it. The Augustan poets had looked at the natural world, certainly, but 'Observation only looked out of a window' (*Notebook*) — their response to what they saw in nature was different from the more celebrated perceptions of the Romantics, but as original. As early as 1730 Thomson had established that nature was a subject worthy of epic treatment by the poet with *The Seasons*. No poet before Thomson had thought to select as a subject the appearance of the countryside as the seasons change. Learning from Thomson, other poets followed, and the subject became so familiar that it is difficult to appreciate now the novelty of Augustan nature poetry. Elizabeth Barrett herself wrote a moralising poem, 'The Autumn', in 1838, which echoes Thomson in detail if not in intention. Thomson, Collins and Shenstone handle the landscape in poetry in different ways, but all of them bring to their task new insights and perceptions that prepare the literary scene for *Lyrical Ballads*. Elizabeth Barrett writes with the impatience of an initiate when she implicitly contrasts Shenstone with Wordsworth. She had written in her notebook of Shenstone:

> His communion with solitary nature has lit up his spirit with no holy enthusiasm; he is as ineffectually pastoral as if he had spent his life in town ... My romantic Fleet Street Bard, I wot, who has his ideas of animate nature from Smithfield, and vegetable life from Covent Garden market, might say so much.
> (*Notebook*)

Shenstone ('Poor Shenstone!') 'stands as a contrary example' to all great poets, among whom Wordsworth is prime. For Shenstone and the Augustans, Nature is seen with the vision of a landscape painter. For Wordsworth and the other poets of this revolutionary time, Nature is a nurturing spirit and inspirational force, a kind of catalyst through which all that is best in a man is realised. Wordsworth's response to nature, recollected in the remembrance of some of his own most significant experiences, produces universal perceptions of humanity and the natural world. 'Let nature be your teacher', Wordsworth had urged, for

> One impulse from a vernal wood
> May teach you more of man,

Of moral evil and of good,
Than all the sages can.
('The Tables Turned', 21-4)

Elizabeth Barrett had learned the lesson from *Tintern Abbey*, from *The Excursion* ('a philosophical poem, containing views on Man, Nature and Society'), from poems like 'Nutting', and the poem she admired above all, *Intimations of Immortality*. Wordsworth's gospel became her creed. As she wrote in the *Athenaeum*:

Let a poet never write the words 'tree', 'hill', 'river', and he may still be true to nature. Nature is where God is! ... Nature is a larger meaning.

Elizabeth Barrett's nature poems such as 'A Sea-Side Walk' and 'Man and Nature' and 'A Poet's Vow' and 'Mountaineer and Poet' all contain unmistakable Wordsworthian echoes, though she may sometimes vary in her reading of the final significance of nature; but she is never in doubt about its 'larger meaning'. Wordsworth's further influence is clear in important poems like 'The Lost Bower' and 'Hector in the Garden'. *Tintern Abbey* and *Intimations of Immortality* both concern, of course, the poet's retrospective look at his childhood, or more youthful years, and their place in his awareness of nature and the development of his mind. He feels wistful regret that nature means to him as a mature adult something different from then, but he acknowledges that the years have brought compensations that outweigh the animal appreciation of times past — now his relation with nature is established with 'the philosophic mind', now 'Our Souls have sight of that immortal sea/Which brought us hither' (*Intimations of Immortality*, 156-7).

'The Lost Bower' and 'Hector in the Garden' are born of Romantic theory and culture. They are set in the days of Elizabeth Barrett's Herefordshire childhood, in the green land of the Malvern hills, 'where my daily/Steps in jocund childhood played,' and both concern the significance of childhood experiences in the shaping of the adult mind. The bower has been the birthplace of poetic aspiration, the beginning of the quest. The child never finds it again but it achieves mythic proportions and symbolic significance in her mind, and the adult poet can look back and say:

In the pleasant orchard-closes,

'God bless all our gains', say we,
But 'May God bless all our losses'
Better suits with our degree ...
('The Lost Bower', 1-4)

And Hector, created lovingly in flowers by the child-gardener,

(Eyes of gentianellas azure,
Staring, winking at the skies:
Nose of gillyflowers and box;
Scented grasses put for locks
Which a little breeze at pleasure
Set a waving round his eyes)
('Hector in the Garden', 49-54)

returns in spirit to encourage the adult poet, the 'neglecter of the present's work unsped' ('Though my past is dead as Hector, /And though Hector is twice dead'[103-8]).

Living as she did where England merges with Wales, Elizabeth Barrett grew up in a land 'Dimpled close with hill and valley, /Dappled very close with shade' ('The Lost Bower'), and this to her was nature and the stuff of poetry, which she experienced alone. Aurora Leigh, fresh from the dramatic landscapes of Tuscany, commented ruefully that the fields and hedges and hills of Herefordshire were more a park than a wilderness, but to Elizabeth Barrett the green hills and 'pleasant orchard closes' were the nature she loved and from which she drew the central images of her early poetry. 'The Lost Bower', for instance, an important poem from an early volume, is set firmly in the green land of Langland and Piers Plowman, and the very 'tree-locked valley' of Hope End, with its 'Summer-snow of apple blossoms running up from shade to shade'. She wrote later to Hugh Boyd, 'The subject of the poem was an actual fact of my childhood' (LB, 266), and she told Mrs Martin 'The scene of that poem is the wood above the garden at Hope End' (L,1,10 September 1844).

It is a poem, like so many of Elizabeth Barrett's, about poetry and her conception of her own position as a poet. She grew up at a time when traditional ideas of poetry were being challenged and re-evaluated: Wordsworth and the school he represented had forced readers of poetry to rethink the traditional concepts that had defined poets of the eighteenth century, and young poets like Elizabeth

Barrett who had absorbed Wordsworth through every pore had responded excitedly to the vision.

'The Lost Bower' has every association with Wordsworth and his school, though it speaks with its own voice too. It is a quest poem of a young poet in search of the source of her own creativity, which she identifies as located in a 'bower of beauty', a hallowed spot described in Chinese-box-like terms. On the outside are the 'Malvern hills, for mountains counted/Not unduly ...' (43-4) which in turn enclose 'the wood, all close and clenching/Bough in bough and root in root' (51-2), which defines the poetic quest of the traveller as she confronts and battles with the obstacles of her art. But she takes courage from former poets who have successfully fought their way:

> And the poets wander, said I,
> Over places all as rude;
> Bold Rinaldo's lovely lady
> Sat to meet him in a wood ...
>
> And if Chaucer had not travelled
> Through a forest by a well,
> He had never dreamt nor marvelled
> At those ladies fair and fell ...
>   (60-74)

and concludes

> Thus I thought of the old singers
> And took courage from their song,
> Till my little struggling fingers
> Tore asunder gyve and thong
> Of the brambles which entrapped me, and the barrier
>   branches strong.
>   (76-80)

She labours painfully through the threatening forest until in the very middle of it she reaches the end of her quest. 'I stood suddenly astonished — I was gladdened unaware' — the bower of bliss is before her, contained within the centre of the wood.

> But that wood appeared a marvel
> In the wildness of the place;
> With such seeming art and travail,

71

> Finely fixed and fitted was
> Leaf to leaf, the dark green ivy to the summit from the base.
>   (111-115)

> All the floor was paved with glory,
> Greenly, silently inlaid ...
>   (131-2)

Inside the bower she muses on the spirit of the place; but before she has identified it (Nature? Dryad? fairies?), 'Came a sound, a sense of music, which was rather felt than heard' (175), the voice, it seems, of poetry itself. She cannot identify the source or the nature of the music, but absorbs it in a kind of trance:

> I rose up in exaltation
> And an inward trembling heart,
> And (it seemed) in geste of passion
> Dropped the music to my feet
> Like a garment rustling downwards — such a silence
>   followed it!
>   (211-215)

The young poet has attained ultimate ecstasy. But then, as with Keats alone on the mountain side or listening to the fading song of the nightingale, the trance begins to break up: 'Mystic Presences of power / Had upsnatched me to the Timeless, then returned me to the Hour' (219-20), and the life of the everyday returns:

> In a child-abstraction lifted,
> Straightway from the bower I past,
> Foot and soul being dimly drifted
> Through the greenwood, till, at last,
> In the hilltop's open sunshine I all consciously was cast.
>   (221-225)

The vision fades, but the bower is no less real to the poet. She will return, she vows, daily, to listen to the music, to re-experience the ecstasy, to become indeed the very spirit of the bower. But as with Keats, what seems the very reality of now has different intentions: as the vision fades the bower vanishes, 'The next morning all had vanished, or my wandering missed the place', and the Herefordshire hills and forests never yield again the magic bower.

The poet, grown older, reflects ruefully on the passing of her youthful inspiration, describing the vain journeys in search of the elusive source. But she concludes that in spite of seeming so, all is not lost. Life is made up of such seeming losses, and the loss of the bower 'did prefigure /Other loss of better good' (291-292). Other losses followed, in fact, of pleasures, and hopes, and health, 'But the first of all my losses was the losing of the bower'. Yet the finding, and its significance, are more important, and they are not lost.

All the echoes of Wordsworth are there in this Hope End poem. 'Nutting' is the parallel that comes to mind at once, though the poet's intentions there may be different. But the bower visited by the child is the same in both. Wordsworth's 'green and mossy bower' represents the same sacred grove as Elizabeth Barrett's 'green lusus, fashioned half in/Chance and half in Nature's play' (238-239), each of them representing unexpected aspects of the poet's mind, each of them the habitation of the spirit of poetry. Verbal echoes of Wordsworth and Coleridge sound in lines and phrases throughout the poem (Elizabeth Barrett always thought Coleridge 'the grander genius', 'a soul more intensely poetical in the appreciation of mind than the author of *The Excursion* ...' [LB, 254]). The whole poem, of course, with its nostalgic retrospect to the days of childhood and the visions of innocence, echoes Wordsworth's 'things which I have seen I now can see no more'. Elizabeth Barrett searches vainly for her bower as the years pass, but 'nevermore upon it turned [her] mortal countenance', and she acknowledges with Wordsworth that with maturity a glory has 'past from the earth'. But like Wordworth's *Intimations*, 'The Lost Bower' is not negative, merely wistful. Wordsworth had said

> Though nothing can bring back the hour
> Of splendour in the grass, of glory in the flower;
> We will grieve not, rather find
> Strength in what remains behind ...
>   (*Intimations of Immortality*, 183-6)

Years, though they had witnessed 'something that is gone', had brought in compensation the philosophic mind. Elizabeth Barrett's experience is something similar. The quest for the bower, though it cannot be repeated, is complete. The music for which she sought the source is discovered in the sense of music 'rather felt than heard', which falls round her like a fountain, and is to be always her source of inspiration. The bower is not really lost, but is to be revisited through the imagination:

> Hark! my spirit in it prayeth
> Through the sunshine and the frost.
> And the prayer preserves it freely, to the last and uttermost.
> (363-5)

Not that 'The Lost Bower' was the first of the quest poems in which the young Elizabeth Barrett explores her identity as a poet. Years before she had used the same imagery drawn from the scenes round Hope End to consider the source of inspiration in 'The Deserted Garden', a similarly Wordsworthian poem. It is more uncertain than 'The Lost Bower', and less mature, but looks back in the same way to the happy child through the perspective of the adult poet (reflecting 'We draw the moral afterward,/We feel the gladness then'). It is the garden in which she and Bro and the other children had played in 'days departed', and it is the 'circle smooth of mossy ground / Beneath a poplar tree' which she had claimed as her own. Her 'bower' there is defined by the garden rose-trees which hedge it in, and the spirit of the place is a 'lady proud' who used to come there, the poet speculates, to muse on 'science or love's compliment'. But the happy child is already preparing for her vocation in life, and has no such thoughts. She builds a 'hermit-house' to which she takes water from the spring and 'cresses glassy wet' and pretends to be the 'gentle hermit of the dale' of whom she is reading in the books she takes to her sanctuary:

> For oft I read within my nook
> Such minstrel stories; till the breeze
> Made sounds poetic in the trees,
> And then I shut the book.
> (473-6)

Years have passed since the child played by herself in the deserted garden and imagined herself the characters in Ariosto and the other minstrels, and she reflects sadly on the change. The garden is deserted once again; and the gladness she read of and enjoyed there is proved different by experience.

It was nearly six years since the Barretts had left Hope End, but she still thought of it longingly:

My childhood from my life is parted,
My footsteps from the moss which grew
Its fairy circle round: anew
The garden is deserted.
  (81-84)

The publication of *The Seraphim, and Other Poems* in which 'The Deserted Garden' appeared, marked something of a turning point in Elizabeth Barrett's life. The volume appeared in May 1838, and was the first to be published in her own name. In June the Barretts moved to their first permanent home since Hope End, to 50 Wimpole Street, and there a new phase was to begin.

But the influence of Wordsworth, experienced in youth at Hope End, was to remain with her wherever she was writing. Wordsworth is obviously in the poet's mind in *Aurora Leigh*, Elizabeth Barrett's masterpiece, which follows Wordsworth's *The Prelude* in time and theme. Both are the autobiographies of a poet: Wordsworth called *The Prelude* 'The Growth of a Poet's Mind', while in *Aurora Leigh* Elizabeth Barrett gives us knowledge of human nature and a more comprehensive soul than that of ordinary people.

'The Poet's soul was with me at that time', Wordsworth was to write in *The Prelude*, 'Sweet meditations, the still overflow of present happiness'; and Elizabeth Barrett wrote in an early poem in 1838, less memorably but as self-consciously, of the poet, 'Neath a golden cloud he stands, / Spreading his impassioned hands':

He a poet! Know him by
The ecstasy-dilated eye,
Not uncharged with tears that ran
Upward from his heart of man;
By the cheek, from hour to hour,
Kindled bright or sunken wan
With a sense of lonely power;
By the brow, uplifted higher
Than others, for more low declining:
By the life which words of fire
Overboiling have burned white
While they gave for nations light ...
    ('Earth and Her Praisers', 105-115)

as she experienced the exhilaration and the burden of the sublime office.

She was still musing on the nature and position of the poet later, when she responded to Carlyle's idea of 'the poet as hero' in *Aurora Leigh*. Wordsworth had spoken of the poet as divinely inspired (and Elizabeth Barrett followed in 'Earth and her Praisers'); Carlyle, a generation later, defines the poet as one who has 'penetrated ... to the sacred mystery of the Universe', a prophet who will communicate God's truth to men. Elizabeth Barrett speaks with him in 'Earth and her Praisers', and twenty years on picks up his tone again in *Aurora Leigh*:

> ... I write so
> Of the only truth-tellers now left to God,
> The only speakers of essential truth,
> Opposed to relative, comparative,
> And temporal truths, the only holders by
> His sun-skirts, through conventional gray glooms;
> The only teachers who instruct mankind
> From just a shadow in a charnel-wall
> To find man's veritable stature out
> Erect, sublime ...
>   (I, 910)

The poet has a new function, but though he is now the channel between man and God, he is still, as he was for Wordsworth, a figure of God-like stature, 'Become divine i' the utterance'. Elizabeth Barrett links the law-givers in her verse.

Wordsworth was kind to the young disciple, and sent her poems; she, in some trepidation, sent him her volume of 1844, including 'Lady Geraldine's Courtship', which contained tributes to Wordsworth, the Poet Laureate, to Tennyson the Laureate-in-waiting, and to the largely unknown poet, Robert Browning. It was a tribute to a fading star, an acknowledgement of the current favourite, and a prophetic salute to a poet to be more important to Elizabeth Barrett than either.

Five:
An Essay on Mind, and What Followed

Elizabeth Barrett, much later and in rueful retrospection, looked back in a letter to R.H. Horne to the publication of *An Essay on Mind* in 1826 when she was twenty as 'long repented of, as worthy of all repentance', deploring, with typical self-deprecation, the 'pertness and pedantry' of her early precocity. Pedantic the poems may be called, but pert is hardly the appropriate comment to describe the manner in which she explores, in poem after poem, the nature and role of the poet, and her own ambitions and self-doubts. But the actual appearance of the volume was of the utmost importance in her life, in terms of her own poetic development, and because from it sprang some of the most significant encounters she was ever to make.

It was her first published book (*The Battle of Marathon* had merely been privately printed), though the expenses of publication had been undertaken by the friend of the family Miss Trepsack, or 'Treppy'. It is the first poem in which she tries her own voice and attempts to establish her own identity as a poet, and it is an ambitious, self-confident work. In it she surveys all the different branches of knowledge known to man — Philosophy, History, Science, Metaphysics — and concludes with Poetry,

> where Philosophy would fear to soar
> Young Poesy's elastic steps explore! ...
> For Poesy's whole essence, when defined,
> Is elevation of the reasoning mind'),
> (*Essay on Mind*, 900-902; 945-946)

and a hymn to freedom and Greece. It is very much a poem about poetry and her own ambition to be a poet. 'And oh!' she implores the creative imagination:

> ... while thus the spirit glides away, —
> Give to the world its memory with its clay!
> Some page our country's grateful eyes may scan;
> Some useful truth to bless surviving man;
> Some name to honest bosoms justly dear;
> Some grave, t'exalt the thought and claim the tear.
>   (1253-1258)

Although it is heavily indebted to Pope and Milton in form, the thought is personal: the poem shows the young poet's poetic and intellectual development as she labours in her vocation. Reviewers thought well of it: the *Eclectic Review* found it 'the essay of no ordinary mind — that it discovers considerable talents, informed by extensive reading, no-one, we think, can hesitate to admit', and the *Literary Gazette* concurred. 'This poem', they said gravely, 'is represented to be the production of a young lady and ... we see much to admire'. Elizabeth Barrett's family was fervent in its admiration. 'You are launched on the world as Authoress', declared her mother.

Elizabeth Barrett appreciated the esteem with which her work was received; but what she wanted even more than praise was the criticism of like minds, and discussion with fellow-poets who would understand and share all the difficulties of her vocation. Her life at Hope End was a lonely one, and she felt with growing intensity the frustration of her seclusion remote from the literary world. Her family was loyal and supportive, but could not offer her what she craved most, the sympathy of equals. Her father, whose good opinion she valued almost above all others, showed his limits as a critic when he urged her not to be over-ambitious, not to overreach herself. This was in a judgement of a poem that followed the *Essay on Mind*: the poem was withdrawn and only published after her death, and then in a different form. Her mother, though always a sympathetic audience and reader, was humbler in her claims as a critic, and greeted Elizabeth's published work with undiscriminating enthusiasm. Her adored brother Edward, the like mind with whom she shared every thought and literary ambition in childhood, had left her for school at thirteen, and they were never as close thereafter, for when he returned as a young man, after the crucial period of development, their interests had diverged.

But even as she fretted, with the appearance of her first work came the dawning apprehension of a world outside her family, who might offer what they could not. The first hint was in a letter of congratulation from Uvedale Price, from his home in nearby Foxley, commending her scholarship. Elizabeth Barrett was gratified: Uvedale Price, as well as being an eminent theorist of landscape gardening and 'the picturesque', was also a classical scholar of European renown, whose enthusiasm was for his own theories of the pronunciation of classical Greek. Elizabeth Barrett thanked him for his praise of the *Essay*, but asked him urgently for criticism of her poetry. Uvedale Price complied with a critical commentary of the *Essay*, to which she responded eagerly, picking up every point where his reading of the poem differed from hers, arguing and demonstrating her case with examples from authors ancient and modern, with the ease of a mature scholar. Startled but pleased, Uvedale Price continued the dialogue, and invited Elizabeth Barrett to visit him at Foxley. She was always uneasy when confronted with such a situation, but not even her almost pathological shyness could finally deter her from the pleasure of a more intimate acquaintance with a distinguished writer who took her seriously, and she visited him at his home in Foxley more than once. Uvedale Price, though old enough to be her grandfather, supplied Elizabeth Barrett with the two things she wanted most at this stage in her professional life, namely, a serious and sympathetic audience from whom she might expect and receive instruction, and the stimulus of a like mind. They kept up a lively correspondence on Greek metres, and Elizabeth Barrett happily and proudly agreed to read and comment on his essay on Greek pronunciation before it went to the publisher. Conversely Uvedale Price, who came a baronet in 1828, would listen when she talked, and would understand what she was saying in a way that nobody at Hope End could. She wrote gratefully of his function in her life on his eightieth birthday:

> When the tone faltering grew, — the lamp unbright, —
> Thou didst not still the harp, nor quench the light;
> But patient of my lay, — its harshness borne, —
> Didst spare the minstrel's fault, the critic scorn!

When he died in the fullness of years in 1829 it was as this friendly audience that she missed him most. She wrote honouring him as both landscape theorist and arbitrator of the pronunciation of classical Greek:

Thou spakest once; and every pleasant sight,
Woods waving wild, and fountains gushing bright,
Cool copses, grassy banks, and all the dyes
Of shade and sunshine gleamed before our eyes.
Thou spakest twice; and every pleasant sound
The ancient silken harmony unwound.
    ('To the Memory of Sir Uvedale Price Bart.', 41-46)

'Mr Price's friendship', she wrote, 'has given me more continued happiness than any single circumstance ever did — and I pray for him as the grateful pray.'

But an even more significant admirer than Uvedale Price wrote to her in the months following the publication of the *Essay on Mind*. In the spring of 1827, as she reached twenty-one, she received a letter from a man who was to dominate her life for the next five years: Hugh Stuart Boyd. Their ways were to diverge as events overtook the Barrett family generally and Elizabeth in particular, but his life and hers remained at some level intertwined until his death in 1848, and in the early years of their friendship he was to have a role in her life of the utmost importance.

Boyd was a scholar and a poet. He was also blind. As a peripatetic gentleman of independent means, he moved restlessly round the country with his wife and daughter as the whim took him, and was living at this time near Malvern, not far from Hope End. He had encountered the *Essay on Mind* with enthusiasm, and wrote to his young neighbour to congratulate her on her achievement. Elizabeth Barrett responded in the same terms with which she had replied to Uvedale Price, imploring not compliments but criticism from which she might learn. Hugh Boyd complied. Elizabeth Barrett wrote back. The subjects of their correspondence widened. They went on to exchange letter after letter of argument and discussion on points of theology and Greek scholarship, as well as poetics.

It was of particular significance in Elizabeth Barrett's life that Boyd was the first man outside the family with whom she was to pursue a serious independent relationship. Uvedale Price was known to her family, and she visited him and corresponded with him as a family friend, and with their full approval. Boyd was different. Though her family and Boyd's were later on visiting terms, and exchanged polite gifts (and his daughter occasionally stayed at Hope End as Elizabeth's 'friend') the important relationship was always between Elizabeth Barrett and Boyd. The Barrett family never really understood or unreservedly approved of her relationship with the blind scholar, nor of her need for his company.

Superficially the positions of Hugh Boyd and Uvedale Price were similar. Though without the international standing of Uvedale Price, Boyd was a scholar, and had written Greek tragedies and published translations which more than fulfilled Elizabeth Barrett's requirements for a like mind. He sent her copies of his books, soliciting comment: she sent him the *Jewish Expositor* containing her early published poems. In the early days the relationship was conducted exclusively on paper, where Elizabeth was happiest. She declined to meet him, in spite of his repeated invitations, on the grounds of the distance, her health, and that her father forbade it:

> My father has represented to me that, whatever gratification and improvement I might receive from a personal intercourse with you, yet, as a female, and a young female, I could not pay such a first visit as the one you proposed to me without overstepping the established observance of society ...
> (LB, 11)

though equally important without doubt was her own fatal shyness. But for nearly a year they never met, though living scarcely five miles apart. Their first meeting finally came eleven months after Boyd's first letter when Elizabeth, properly chaperoned, called on him at his house near Malvern, Ruby Cottage and that after a series of accidents and misunderstandings more like musical comedy than Greek tragedy. Once the precedent was set however, regular visits followed. Boyd was a few years older than her father; but Elizabeth records in a letter to her grandmother soon after the meeting:

> My eccentric friend is rather a young-looking man than otherwise, moderately tall, and slightly formed. His features are good — his face very pale, with an expression of placidity and mildness. He is totally blind ... His voice is very harmonious and gentle and low — and seems to have naturally a melancholy cadence and tone! ... I did not see him smile once ...
> (*Diary*, xxi)

What Boyd made of Elizabeth, or what his family thought, no record survives to say. She was barely twenty-two, dark, pretty and five feet tall, and quickly saw herself as embracing the role of helpmeet to her blind master — a living amalgamation of Dorothea Brooke

81

and Milton's daughters. She would read to him, read Greek with him (or listen to him declaim from his phenomenal memory), learn all she could from him of literature and poetry, and talk to him of her work and and his. Boyd himself, in spite of his blindness, was undoubtedly conscious of the possible implications of their relationship, and had clearly defined the limits of the subjects allowed between them — 'No confidences!', he had said, and their exchanges were all on theology, literature, politics, poetry, Greek and the Church Fathers. Unless he sometimes called her 'Porsonia', he called her 'Miss Barrett' until the day nearly twenty years later when they lived in separate parts of London, and she implored him not to, signing herself affectionately thereafter 'Elibet'.

So might the understanding of the relationship have remained, of a spirited but dutiful and admiring pupil on the one side, and a warmly proud but lofty teacher on the other. It is a happy and relaxed picture of an association of like minds, of comradeship where the separate roles are defined and accepted. But some years ago a remarkable manuscript came to light in a London solicitor's office, a notebook bound in paper and labelled in the hand of Robert Browning 'Diary by EBB', which throws light on what was really happening in Elizabeth Barrett's mind during this period of tutelage. It was finally published in 1969.

It is the only diary she ever kept, and it covers one tempestuous year, from early June 1831 to late April 1832 — the time when the Barrett fortune failed and Hope End was sold to strangers, and when Hugh Boyd was the most important person in Elizabeth Barrett's life. It is a fresh, intimate, spontaneous record of the feelings never articulated in their constant correspondence, and though it records (invaluably) all the domestic routine, the social engagements, the political interests and the religious life of a wealthy pre-Victorian family, at the centre of it all is Boyd and her feelings for him, so different from those implied or expressed with such control in her regular letters, until this discovery the only source of such information. Where the letters are balanced, dispassionate, witty, the diary (for she has vowed to be truthful in her record) rages with anguished questioning and the torments of jealousy and suspected slights. Does Mr Boyd enjoy her visits? (Her family have doubted it.) Will she be asked to dine when she calls, and will Mrs Boyd be there? Does Mr Boyd take the same pleasure in the company of Miss Steers or Miss Mushet or Miss Hurd as in hers? ('The society of that Miss

Hurd is as much valued as mine — as much! at least as much! and yet is it probable or possible at her friendship is like my friendship?' 'Eliza told me ... that Miss Steers walks out with Mr Boyd whenever she can. So he is not so considerate to her as he once was to another person!! He is not afraid of disgracing her by his slovenly appearance!!', [*Diary*, 21].) Will Mr Boyd mind if she leaves Hope End? Might he think of moving from Malvern to be near wherever they settle?

She writes her journal every day, and there is scarcely an entry without a reference to Boyd. The diary opens with an extended reflection on the difficulty of her relationship with his daughter Annie, and a rueful question as to whether Boyd's 'regard for me is dependent on his literary estimation of me, and not great enough for me to afford the loss of any part of it' (*Diary*, 3) when she fears Boyd did not like the verses she had published in *The Times*; and it concludes with Boyd's invitation that she beg her father let her 'see him for two or three days' during the turmoil of the sale of Hope End. She writes to him in a letter later, 'I should like ... to say — how much your seeming to wish me to spend two or three days at Ruby Cottage gratified me ... It gave me as much pleasure as anything could give me ...' (LB, 164).

She berates herself for her dependence on his good opinion, reproaches herself for the pain his seeming indifference causes her, but cannot prevent herself scrutinising and analysing his every response. She is impatient with herself at how easily she can feel hurt at Boyd's fancied neglect or careless thoughtlessness. When Miss Steers interrupts them in a reading of Blomfield's edition of *The Seven Chiefs* she admits her annoyance that Boyd presses her to stay; and when he explains later that he did so merely because 'he fancied it would please her to talk longer with me', Elizabeth Barrett says ruefully to herself 'for the thousand and first time I owned myself ... a fool!' (*Diary*, 26).

As the sale of Hope End becomes more and more certain, one thought is uppermost:

> Shall I ask Mr Boyd if he will endeavour to go where we go in the case of our going at all? It would be a comfort for me to know if he would make the endeavour ... Did he not tell me that if I had left Hope End ... 'he would have been happier at Cheltenham than at Malvern, for one reason — because at Cheltenham there was nothing to remind him of my going to

see him'. Must he not care a good deal for me to feel that? ...
What a consolation it would be to me not to leave ... the dearest
and most valued friend I have in the world!!
(*Diary*, 13)

And should the unthinkable happen and Hope End were sold, 'If
Mr Boyd were to follow us, the bearing would be a less hard task —
but I must not lean too many of my hopes on that ... If he cared for
me as I care for him, he would speak and act only in one way'
(*Diary*, 17).

What Boyd was doing, or failing to do, throughout this anguished
time was only what he had undertaken to do; namely to read with
her and teach her. But Elizabeth Barrett looked for more, and her
frustrations and conflicts make the drama of the diary. Not all her
experiences were unhappy, of course. The regular hours she spent
with him in Malvern, at Ruby Cottage or Woodland Lodge, the
house he leased there subsequently, were also times of intense
happiness as they read Aeschylus, Plato, Homer, and the Church
Fathers Gregory, Chrysostom, and Basil. Often she shared meals
with him and occasionally she stayed the night. 'I had wished Mr
Boyd good bye — and had put on my hat, and was tying my cloak,
when Annie proposed my staying all night. I resisted, — she insisted
— And my heart let go its hold in a moment! — the temptation was
too great! — Wrote a note to Bummy, and sent away the carriage,'
though the following morning she was torturing herself with the
dread that as they read Gregory together, 'He was fancied to be cool
in his manner towards me' (*Diary*, 162). One golden time the visit
was an extended one of two and a half weeks, during which they
lived, Boyd records, 'in clover', and read 'somewhat more than 2200
lines together'. All in all she looked back on the time as an idyll, and
wrote to the old man much later, 'the hours spent with you appear
to me some of the happiest of my life' (LB, 179).

When the worst did happen and Hope End was sold, and the
Barretts were to leave Herefordshire, Boyd had already moved on.
He had been willing to make his plans fit in with theirs, as anxious
as Elizabeth Barrett not to forego the pleasures of their literary
companionship, but, balked by Mr Barrett's indecision, he had acted
for himself and moved to Bath some months before. The separation
did not in fact last: within a few months Boyd had followed them to
Sidmouth with his family, and Elizabeth Barrett attempted to take

up the interrupted relationship. After Boyd's departure from Malvern she had abandoned her diary ('in such a crisis of self-disgust that there was nothing for me but to leave off the diary' (LRH, 5 October 1843) and the relationship must be inferred from letters.

The relationship had changed, and was to change further as their paths diverged (the Boyds only stayed a year in Sidmouth), and was never again the charged and passionate obsession of the Hope End years. Elizabeth Barrett, especially after the subsequent move to London, had new friends and new experiences, and began to establish her own identity as a poet. Her feelings towards Boyd were always of warm affection and gratitude for what he had been in the period of her intensest development; but her obsessive yearning for his regard, and her vulnerability to his fancied slights, had gone. She gradually came to assume the role of pitying protector. In her *Poems* of 1844, the first volume of undoubted success with both critics and public, one poem, 'Wine of Cyprus', is specifically dedicated to him. They had shared the drink; and the lines recall the golden hours they had spent together at Ruby Cottage:

> As Ulysses' old libation
> Drew the ghosts from every part,
> So your Cyprus wine, dear Grecian,
> Stirs the Hades of my heart.
> And I think of those long mornings
> Which my heart goes far to seek,
> When, betwixt the folio's turnings,
> Solemn flowed the rhythmic Greek:
> Past the pane the mountain spreading,
> Swept the sheep's-bell's tinkling noise,
> While a girlish voice was reading,
> Somewhat low for ai's and oi's.
>
> Then, what golden hours were for me!
> While we sat together there.
> How the white vests of the chorus
> Seemed to wave up a live air!
> How the cothurns trod majestic
> Down the deep iambic lines,
> And the rolling anapaestic
> Curled like vapour over shrines.
> ('Wine of Cyprus', 61- 80)

She reviews the gallery of great names they have read together —

Aeschylus, Sophocles, Euripides, Plato, and 'your noble Christian bishops, who mouthed grandly the last Greek' (101-102) — and concludes gently:

> Is it not right to remember
> All your kindness, friend of mine,
> When we two sat in the chamber,
> And the poets poured us wine?
> (165-168)

For Boyd himself the relationship with his young pupil and friend became the central fact of his existence. He cared for Elizabeth Barrett, she told Robert later, 'far more than for his own only daughter', and in his later widowed and lonely state, her letters — fewer than in the intense years at Hope End, but still, until her marriage, regular — were shafts of light in his dark world.

And he was to retain a special position in her life. After her secret, hasty marriage with Robert Browning, it was to the home of 'my dearest Mr Boyd' in St John's Wood that she returned, and Boyd who sustained her with bread and butter and wine. It was their last meeting, for less than two years later Boyd died. Elizabeth Barrett, married and far away in Florence, paid tribute to his memory in three sonnets, 'His Blindness', 'His Death', and 'Legacies'.

Hugh Boyd may have been the most significant result of the *Essay on Mind* in terms of her emotional life, and her delayed development from girl to woman, but the most important contact socially and professionally to spring from her first book was undoubtedly John Kenyon. He was remotely related to her through the West Indian connections which they shared, and had met her father at Cambridge, and on the strength of this he wrote to her with congratulations on the appearance of the *Essay*.

John Kenyon was a wealthy London dilettante who knew everybody and spent his life visiting, entertaining and travelling, and in acts of philanthropy. His warm interest in his young cousin, begun with the *Essay* in Hope End days, was to last all his life. After her marriage he stood in place of a father to her, made an annual allowance to her and Browning on the birth of their son, and on his death left both her and Robert enough money to make them financially secure for the rest of their lives. At this stage, however, it was his cousin's burgeoning success as a poet which engaged him. He was immersed in the arts, and wrote poetry himself, and when the family came into residence at their first London home in Gloucester Place in 1835, he did his best to see that she had the chance to make an appearance in the literary world, and to be part of the circle she had longed for wistfully in the solitude of Hope End. His home in Harley Street was a centre of literary life in the capital, where he entertained the distinguished. Carlyle, Monkton Milnes, Tennyson, Crabb Robinson, Landor and Wordsworth are all mentioned as visitors at this time. So to Elizabeth came invitations to soirées, concert parties, dinners and other social occasions, and although both her health and her shyness prevented her from taking full advantage of these benefits, she did meet a number of people of moment either at Kenyon's house or through his means.

The most celebrated, undoubtedly, was Wordsworth, whom she venerated like a god. Conquering her shyness, she sat next to him at dinner in Harley Street, and announced on her return to Gloucester Place, 'I never walked in the skies before; and perhaps never shall again, when so many stars are out!'. Wordsworth remembered the young disciple, encouraged her work, read the poems she sent him, and once even sent her his own.

The day before her meeting with Wordsworth however, Kenyon had arranged that Elizabeth Barrett make the acquaintance of another celebrity, Mary Russell Mitford, who for the next ten years was to be a central point in her life. Mary Mitford was in London for a week, and Kenyon organised a visit to the zoo in Regent's Park so that the two should meet. Mary Mitford was much the elder (she was nearly fifty on the May day in 1836 when the expedition to the zoo took place), but was the literary contact Elizabeth Barrett was looking for, and something of a kindred spirit. She was unmarried and, like the younger woman, was the main emotional resource of her widowed father. She had gained fame with her astonishingly successful series of sketches *Our Village*, which had appeared in the *Lady's Magazine* in 1819, reaching a much wider audience in volume form later. She was also known as a novelist, dramatist and editor, and at the time of the meeting was a very popular writer. She offered the literary companionship which Boyd had provided at Hope End, and the critical audience which Elizabeth Barrett craved now as then.

Their relationship after daily meetings in the week that followed the zoo visit was largely epistolary. Mary Mitford lived with her father in a village near Reading, and was only occasionally in London. For ten years, however, until Elizabeth's marriage, they wrote constantly, often several times a week, whether Elizabeth were in Gloucester Place, Torquay or Wimpole Street. Though their letters covered many topics, literature was an unfailing point in every letter, including books they had read, writers they had met or gossip about them, plays, novels and poetry. It was the opening of a new world for Elizabeth. As she exclaimed to Miss Mitford, until they met there had been 'not a being whom I know here, except Mr Kenyon, who ever says to me, "I care for poetry"' (LM, 7).

It was a lively correspondence, based on genuine affection on both sides. Their tastes and their attitudes were different, for while Elizabeth Barrett saw the role of the artist as all-important, and whose only idea of happiness lay 'deep in poetry and its associations', (LM, xi) Mary Mitford claimed that she 'detested' writing, and found literature 'not at all a healthy occupation' (LM, xi). But there was trust and confidence, and they argued cheerfully. Elizabeth Barrett's attitude in the beginning was of gratified surprise that she, the still unknown, should be recognised and sought after by a literary lion like Mary Russell Mitford 'professing to love me, and asking me to write to her too!' (LM, x). On the other side Miss Mitford quickly came to see her as 'the most remarkable woman probably that ever lived', and wrote to her that

> My love and ambition for you often seems to be more like that of a mother for a son, or a father for a daughter, than the common bonds between of even a close friendship between two women of different ages and similar pursuits. I sit and think of you, and of the poems that you will write, and of that strange brief rainbow crown called Fame, until the vision is before me as vividly as ever a mother's heart hailed the eloquence of a patriot son ...
> (LM, x-xi)

Elizabeth Barrett responded to the genuine kindliness and warmth of Miss Mitford, and she pursued the relationship enthusiastically:

> ... let me try to say how deeply and truly I thank you for all your affectionateness and kindness to me. I believe I am not naturally unsusceptible to affectionateness, even from those for whom I might not otherwise have cared the hum of a bee. That I should be very susceptible to *yours* is *very* natural indeed ...
> (LM, 5)

As well as being the literary contact with whom she could share ideas, Mary Mitford also offered her very practical help with her ambition to be among the circle at the centre of London literary life. Miss Mitford had the task of editing a gift-book for the Christmas market, and asked Elizabeth Barrett to contribute a poem to accompany the picture she sent. Though doubtful in principle of the value of such a project, Elizabeth nevertheless obliged her friend with a ballad, 'The Romance of the Ganges', which accompanied the picture of 'a very charming group of Hindoo girls floating their lamps upon the Ganges' (*Life of Mary Russell Mitford*, 76-77). The system of such gift-books often attracted eminent names as contributors, and Elizabeth Barrett secured valuable space in *Findens' Tableaux* (1838).

As the younger woman matured and her fame and confidence grew the tone of her letters to Mary Mitford was modified. As well as the deference to an older woman who had already succeeded where Elizabeth Barrett aspired, she was able to offer advice and sympathy in Miss Mitford's affairs, her financial problems, her literary projects and the questions that arose with her father Dr Mitford, both before and after his death in 1842. In her own affairs, too, Miss Mitford proved a most instant, practical friend at a very low point in Elizabeth's life, after the tragic death of Bro in 1840, when she offered Flush as a companion in her friend's bereavement. But what concerned them most often was their common love of literature. One passion they shared was for novels, and on this common ground they were happy to disagree on mere differences of taste. While Miss Mitford liked Jane Austen and Mrs Radcliffe, for instance, Elizabeth was obsessed with French novels, Hugo and Georges Sand and Eugene Sue ('Mr Kenyon was quite unaware of your and my ever quarrelling on the subject! ...' 6 July 1843). Elizabeth devoured Richardson, and dares to say she prefers Bulwer Lytton to Scott ('[Scott] is more a painter than a poet. It is an outside view of humanity...' 21 December 1842), they argue amicably over Lever, they agree to differ over the genius of Balzac and Dickens ('To compare Dickens to Balzac as a great artist would be impossible to me. *He* is fathoms below *him* in both power and art' 30 December 1844).

It was the same in poetry. Miss Mitford's real taste was for the poets of the past, for Augustans like Dryden. She deplores the 'originality' of contemporary poetry, and the 'obscurity' of the rising generation. They share a rueful view of the ultimate limitations of the poetesses, L.E.L, Felicia Hemans and Catherine Sedgwick, and Miss Mitford, it seems, can only concur with Elizabeth Barrett's enthusiasm for the acknowledged established masters, Keats and Wordsworth.

She can scarcely understand Elizabeth Barrett's rhapsodies over the present rising star, Tennyson, who is both 'original' and 'obscure'. For Elizabeth Barrett, whose idea of happiness is poetry, obscurity in a poem need be no fault. The fault, if any, lies with the reader, who has failed to approach the sanctum of the poet's mind. Tennyson's poetry, she declares, has 'rapt me in Elysium' with its 'astonishing power of subtle thought in a silver-vibrating language!' (14 December 1842). So has that of the new poet, whose reputation and esteem lag far behind Tennyson's, Mr Browning. His difficulty and obscurity stand in the way of popular appreciation, but from the moment he enters Elizabeth Barrett's consciousness she is his fiercest defender, and her constant topic.

Miss Mitford first brought Browning to Elizabeth's attention. She had met Browning through Kenyon just before she met Elizabeth Barrett, and long before Elizabeth herself met him, and had instantly and almost instinctively disliked him. She wrote to a correspondent after the elopement:

> I met him once as I told you when he had long ringlets and no neckcloth — and seemed to me about the height and size of a boy of twelve years old — Femmelette — is a word made for him. A strange sort of a person to carry such a woman as Elizabeth Barrett off her feet
> (LM, xiii)

Her response to his poetry was unequivocal. She found it 'one heap of obscurity, confusion, and weakness', and never lost an opportunity to speak slightingly of it to her correspondent in Wimpole Street. They talked of *Paracelsus* on that first meeting in 1836, a day after she had met the author. Browning, who had already achieved some notoriety in 1833 with *Pauline*, had barely improved his popular reputation with his long dramatic poem *Paracelsus*, published in 1835, which Miss Mitford dismissed briskly as wilfully obscure. Elizabeth, when she had chance to read the poem, felt differently. True, she conceded that perhaps it lacked something of clearness and concentration, but without question it was the work of a true poet. She wrote a little later to another friend:

> Mr Browning knows thoroughly what a poet's true work is.
> His very obscurities have an oracular nobleness about them
> which pleases me — but passion burns the paper.
>   (LRH, 1 May 1843)

His was a new voice in poetry, which Elizabeth Barrett recognised and responded to with all her heart. Poetry was changing (she was to set it all out in 'The Dead Pan' a few years later) and the future lay with poets like herself, and Tennyson, and Browning. She never had any doubt that Browning was a great poet — she believed unquestioningly in his genius from the first encounter. Though she valued her own growing fame she was irked that the public failed to recognise him for so long. It was not until some time after her own death, however, that Browning's own turn was to come.

What she responded to in particular in Browning's poetry was what she identified as its mysticism. She felt vehemently that 'Every true poet ... has a religious passion in his soul' (LRH, December 1843), and Browning's religion was at the heart of every poem, and matched her own. She was writing shortly to Mrs Martin in Ledbury of letters from Browning, 'King of the mystics' (L, I, January 1845), who, she concedes, is thus only read 'in a peculiar circle very strait and narrow', and urges Mary Mitford to estimate him, as she does, for his 'parables'. But it was a quality to which Miss Mitford was largely unsympathetic, and this aspect of Browning's genius remained inaccessible to her. Religion was an important area in which she and Elizabeth Barrett were in different camps. Where Elizabeth Barrett yearned naturally for the spiritual, Mary Mitford, as in her literary tastes, belonged in this to the eighteenth century, and was robust in her commonsense attitude to the unseen. She belonged to no church but believed vaguely when pressed in 'goodness', and worried Elizabeth considerably. She could not make head or tail of Miss Mitford's position and even feared her friend had 'Catholic tendencies' when on a whim Miss Mitford had attended the Roman Catholic chapel instead of the expected Nonconformist kind. Though Elizabeth's own religious life had no need of forms or intermediaries ('I love Christ, and recognise in Him the brotherhood of all Believers ... The church is one, and we, alas! are many!' [Letter to William Merry, 2 November 1843, in *The Religious Opinions of Elizabeth Barrett Browning*, 26]) it was inner and deep, and she recognised a similar mind in Robert Browning.

His poetry is a constant topic in her letters to her friend as volume after volume succeeded *Paracelsus*. One in particular was *Bells and Pomegranates*, which had been appearing throughout 1844. Kenyon made attempts to arrange a meeting between them, but, as usual in the face of a new situation, Elizabeth's courage failed and she produced her trump card, her health. Her own device to attract Browning's attention was in a central poem of her own volume of 1844, 'Lady Geraldine's Courtship'. At the heart of the poem is a tribute to the significant poets of the time, Wordsworth, Tennyson and Browning. The narrator of the poem selects for his reading

> ... a modern volume, Wordsworth's solemn-thoughted idyl,
> Howitt's ballad-verse, or Tennyson's enchanted reverie —
> Or from Browning some 'Pomegranate', which if cut deep
>   down the middle,
> Shows a heart within blood-tinctured, of a veined humanity.
>   (101-104)

Browning, as she had anticipated, read the lines alluding to his *Bells and Pomegranates*, and promptly wrote to thank her for the compliment.

The first letter — from one poet to another — was written 10 January 1845, and the second three days later, on the thirteenth. They were spontaneous, enthusiastic letters full of delight about her poetry and his admiration, in the style which was Browning's own. Elizabeth's replies were demure. She asked, as always, for not compliments but criticism of her work, though this time not from older teachers like Uvedale Price and Hugh Boyd from the Hope End days, but from another poet. Browning complied with some appropriate comments. The letters continued back and forth, and over the weeks the friendship grew, eagerly on his side, more cautiously but no less enthusiastically on hers.

The letters to Mary Mitford slackened noticeably. Only after Browning's second there is the first mention, with studied casualness, of this new friendship:

> ... I have had two delightful letters from Mr Browning — (did
> I tell you?) and I (you know) believe in Mr Browning as a man
> of genius and an original poet ...
>   (15 January 1845)

There is no further mention of the correspondence or of Robert

Browning for several weeks, till

> Mr Browning and I have grown to be devoted friends, I
> assure you — and he writes me letters praying to be let in,
> quite heart-moving and irresistible.
> (18 March 1845)

Browning was clearly anxious to extend their relationship by a meeting.
She resisted his prayers till nearly the end of May. But when the
first visit was actually made, and was instantly followed, to
Elizabeth's appalled dismay, by his proposal of marriage, the account
to Miss Mitford was simply a careless reference wedged between an
announcement of her aunt's projected visit and an acknowledgement of some lines by Clare which her friend had sent:

> ... oh, — did I tell you in my last letter that I had seen lately ...
> Mr Browning? He said in his courtesy more, in the way of
> request, than the thing was worth, — and so I received him
> here one morning, and liked him much.
> (26 May 1845)

Apparently casual remarks in succeeding letters over the next few
weeks are largely of his poetry, though in fact his visits instantly
became weekly, and letters passed between them several times
between each visit. But the sub-text is there, if Miss Mitford had
known how to read it. The summer of 1845 is dominated, we know,
by Elizabeth's growing relationship with Robert Browning, and
almost predictably her health improved dramatically. 'I continue to
gain strength very much, and surprise people who only see me at
intervals ... I was in a carriage the other day and got as far into
Regent's Park as the bridge ... (July 1845). She finds herself 'better
and fitter for travelling than I ever found myself' (September 1845),
and she is in an agony, even, to vary her invalid life by wintering
somewhere warmer, like Malta or Italy.

The doctor agreed ('not merely advised, but enjoined' [September
1845]), but reckoned without Edward Barrett's peremptory veto.
The last time she had wintered outside London was in Torquay in
1840, and in the summer that followed, Bro, his sister's companion,
had drowned there. Mr Barrett did not intend his family to be
divided again. The letters to Mary Mitford are full of Elizabeth's
chagrin at this decision, but still say little of Browning, who was as

enthusiastic as she was for the winter's release from Wimpole Street, and was undoubtedly one motive for her wish.

The threat of what was in fact incipient does not loom until the following autumn. By this time the relationship between the couple had passed — without a hint to the unsuspecting Miss Mitford, hitherto her confidante — from Elizabeth's affrighted response to Robert's ill-timed proposal to the position where they were 'Dearest' to each other, and Robert was even at one point determined to confront Mr Barrett with their position. Their plans to be married were checked at the last minute by her father's sudden edict that the whole household immediately leave London while 50 Wimpole Street was papered and decorated: their solution was to bring forward the date they had planned to the weekend following the edict — and they were married secretly on 12 September at St Marylebone Church.

The first hint to Miss Mitford, which she was only to understand in retrospect, came in a letter of 14 September asking that she defer a visit on Wednesday, and begging for her sympathy and understanding — 'your indulgence even, perhaps', for 'I have a great deal to tell you'. The letter that followed on 18 September explained it all:

> ... [When] you read this letter I shall have given to one of the most gifted and admirable of men a wife unworthy of him. I shall be the wife of Robert Browning ... He has loved me for nearly two years, and said so at the beginning. I would not listen. I could not believe even ... He overcame me at last ... The truth became obvious that he would be happier with me than away from me, and I ... why, I am only as any woman in the world, with a heart belonging to her ... I was a woman and shall be a wife when you read this letter ... We go to Italy ... Try to think of me gently and if you can bear to write to me, let me hear at Orleans — Poste Restante.

Without question Miss Mitford was devastated. Nothing had prepared her for the coup. Their differing views and estimates of Browning and Browning's poetry were something of a joke between them, but one point on which they had never it seemed disagreed, except for the sake of argument, was that of marriage. Miss Mitford, a single woman with pronounced views on the married state (marriages, she wrote, 'are the most foolish things under the sun' [LM, xiii]), adopted the extreme position; Miss Barrett liked to argue a modified case, that a happy marriage was the happiest state, but observed that such marriages scarcely existed. As late as February 1846 she had written to her friend '*Marriage in the abstract*, has always seemed to me the most profoundly indecent of all ideas — and I never could make out how women, mothers and daughters, could talk of it as setting up a trade ...'. Her *volte face* later the same year required some justification: her long letter of explanation goes on

> As to marriage, it never was high up in my ideal ... I never could have married a common man ... I thought always that a man whom I could love would never stoop to love me.
> (18 September 1845)

But this 'man of genius and marvellous attainments — and of a heart and spirit above them all' has contradicted all the views of a lifetime, and persuaded her that their life together will justify their act.

Elizabeth Barrett (now Browning) was conscious, of course, of the blow the act would prove to her friend, and the sense of desolation she must feel. In an attempt to alleviate the pain of the betrayal she added in her letter:

> It would have been wrong against [Mr Kenyon] and against you to have told either of you ... If I had loved you less, dearest Miss Mitford, I could have told you sooner.
> (ibid.)

Miss Mitford had little option but to make the best of the situation and conceal the hurt as best she might. She did in fact write to the Brownings at Orleans, a brave letter of loving sympathy, saying she approved of what had happened, and would have been glad to stand by Elizabeth at the church, if asked. Elizabeth was reassured by the letter, and by Kenyon's, which heartily endorsed the decision they had made. The response from her friends went some way towards comforting her in the face of her father's (and brothers') ominous resentment at the slight she had offered them in her unconventional marriage. But at least the correspondence with Miss Mitford — one link with the past — could be maintained, and their old relationship continued in spite of the jar it had sustained.

It was a different kind of relationship, of course, but Miss Mitford recognised ruefully that it was in her own interests to accept it on Elizabeth's terms. A few weeks after the wedding she wrote:

> The people who know Mr Browning well seem to like him
> much ... and it is so much in my interest to think well of him,
> and his dear wife writes of him so magnificently, that I hope
> in time to forgive even his stealing her away.
> (LM, xv)

So they corresponded freely. Elizabeth wrote about her new life in Italy, about Robert, about Pen, about her work. But they wrote less about their earlier subjects — gossip from the literary world, the books they were reading, Flush. Their old intimacy was gone, and the breach in their confidence was never totally repaired, though they still met occasionally in London whenever the Brownings visited there.

Her death in 1855 was the snapping of another link between the old life and the new, and Elizabeth felt it keenly. Miss Mitford was one of the 'tutors' who had known her as an obscure fledgling poet scarcely emerged from Hope End and the apprentice work of the *Essay on Mind*. She owed her debts of many kinds, and she acknowledged it.

Six:
'Themes for Poets' Uses'

Elizabeth Barrett explored the great verities in her poetry: religion, politics, and above all, love. They are time-honoured themes in literature perhaps, but in the turbulent times in which she lived all these conventional topics for the poet had arrived at some significant stage of development — and the poet must be part of what was happening in society. It was the role of poets, as Elizabeth Barrett saw it, to call the attention of society to issues as they unfolded, and to influence the course of development by what they wrote. As she expressed it in *Aurora Leigh*, a poet's work is

> to represent the age,
> Their age, not Charlemagne's — this live, throbbing age
> That brawls, cheats, maddens, calculates, aspires,
> And spends more passion, more heroic heat,
> Between the mirrors of its drawing-rooms
> Than Roland with his knights at Rocevalles
> To flinch from modern coat or flounce.
> Cry out for togas and the picturesque
> Is fatal — foolish too.
> (V, 202-10)

The time has come for poetry to deal with modern themes, and to address contemporary issues; for, as she had already commented in 'The Dead Pan',

> Earth outgrows the mythic fancies
> Sung beside her in her youth,
> And those debonair romances
> Sound but dull beside the truth.
> (232-235)

So in the realm of politics, Elizabeth Barrett was an acute observer of Europe, whether from the seclusion of Hope End or in the heart of the capital or as an on-the-spot observer in Italy. Her commentary on international politics runs from her earliest work, but most consciously in the political poetry written in Italy in the cause of the Risorgimento (*Casa Guidi Windows* in two parts, in 1847 and 1851, and then *Poems Before Congress* in 1860) and is, perhaps, as much a celebration of her own liberation as an analysis of Italy's: the political situation there coincides with the start of her own new life as wife and mother as well as poet, of Elizabeth Barrett, 'woman and artist'.

In terms of politics at home, she was as uneasily aware of the problems of life in the cities as most of the great writers, and that one price for England's apparent greatness was the misery and degradation of the poor, on whose exploitation it depended.

> ... Let others shout,
> Other poets praise my land here:
> I am sadly sitting out,
> Praying, 'God forgive her grandeur'.
> ('A Song for the Ragged Schools of London', 21-24)

was her response to this dilemma in one of her last poems.

In matters of faith, like other poets she was appalled by the spiritual emptiness that seemed to mark the time. The received truths of Christianity were challenged in the western world by science and history, and material values apparently reigned supreme. She was anxious to establish in her poetry the ever more pressing need for a spiritual centre for the 'lordly English', and felt, as did others, that poetry had a significant role to play.

And in the field of personal relationships, in particular that between men and women, she was the recorder of the dawning shift in perception of the position of women in society which *Aurora Leigh* expresses and considers so momentously. But the poems for which she has been, perhaps best remembered for most of the twentieth century, *Sonnets from the Portuguese*, are her most personal response to the question of how the sexes interact. They set down the stages of her own growing relationship with Robert Browning, in sonnets which have delighted readers as much for their 'truth' as any other quality, though they stand among the finest of Victorian sonnet sequences.

Other relationships, and other forms of love too, are part of the material of her poetry: the love between parents and children, and brother and sister, and love in the context of politics, or between man and the animal kingdom, all contribute to her theme. And divine love is a recurrent refrain throughout. All the themes mark her work from the beginning, and her handling of them is a rewarding guide to the nature and experience of the writer.

Politics and religion may well be topics never to be discussed in polite society, but they were central issues in the conversation at Hope End, and central subjects in Elizabeth Barrett's poetry and thinking. The Barretts, and the Graham-Clarkes, were public figures involved with national and local events which were changing society, and the burning topics of the day were earnestly discussed in Herefordshire, both as principles and as matters affecting family and friends. Many hints of what was happening in the outside world appear in Elizabeth's diary, her letters, and elsewhere. 1831 and 1832 were, after all, exciting years in Britain and abroad, and the observation of a precociously intelligent, alert witness of events and their significance is likely to be interesting.

In 1832 what people were talking about most was the Reform Bill. Edward Barrett's brother Sam, Elizabeth's favourite uncle, had been the Member for Richmond in Yorkshire from 1820 to the time of his return to Jamaica to manage the estate in the early 1830s, and the family was inevitably involved to some degree with parliamentary affairs. The Barretts discussed politics heatedly. Edward Barrett was High Sheriff of the county in 1812 and 1814 and a Freeman of Gloucester, and had been pressed to stand as the (certain) candidate for Herefordshire in 1820. He was, said one commentator, 'a most determined Whig', and in the winter of 1818 became actively involved in parliamentary reform, supporting Robert Price, son of Sir Uvedale, and campaigning widely for him on this ticket. Though Barrett himself declined to stand, he remained fiercely interested in politics all his life, and his young family followed him. He was a regular attender at the debates in the House of Commons whenever he was in London during this period, and he and his sons took a vigorous part in local political meetings, especially at this crucial period in parliamentary history. They were strongly committed to the idea of reform, and made forceful contributions which the local paper reported. The *Herefordshire Journal* of 12 October 1831 speaks enthusiastically of Edward Moulton Barrett's contribution to the debate. Elizabeth (votes for women were nearly a century away) followed the proceedings in parliament in *The Times* and the commentary in the *Quarterly Review*, and wrote anxious letters to Boyd deploring the opposition the Bill was encountering. She noted all the details of the procedure of the Bill in her diary, consternation when it was thrown out in March, jubilation when it passed the second reading in April.

She was always on the reforming side in politics, and behind any smaller nation bidding for independence. Beth's plan is to don armour and 'destroy the Turkish empire, and deliver "Greece the glorious"'; and Elizabeth refers ruefully in her diary to the routing of the Belgian army by the Dutch in a battle during the Belgian struggle for independence in 1831.

When Colonel Stanhope's book on *Greece in 1823 and 1824* appeared, she read it eagerly, particularly the 'pathetic little description of the last moments of Byron addressed to Stanhope by the friend of our poet, Trelawney...', as she records in her notebook. It was a book she said, 'as little published for the uninitiated as for the uninterested', but Elizabeth was neither: she was passionately committed to the cause of Greece, and had already noted reading *The Greek Revolution* — 'I like the book to my soul!'.

Her absorbed interest in foreign affairs was to continue to the end, as she followed the politics of France and even more of Italy from a ringside seat during the fifteen years she lived abroad. She identified closely with the smaller, weaker side, or individual victim, and her enthusiasm was always for whoever she saw as a deliverer.

Her earliest poems run on a constant theme, the struggle of the weak against the strong. Some are hymns to the hero of her childhood, Byron, who had so memorably used his own fame to further the liberty and the independence of Greece, and her earliest published poem was 'Stanzas, Excited by Some Recollections on the Present State of Greece', which appeared in the *New Monthly Review* in 1821, when she was fifteen. 'Stanzas on the Death of Lord Byron' and other poems of her first published collection all celebrate Byron, 'the great Deliverer ... Expiring in the land he only lived to save':

> For his voice resounded through our land
> Like the voice of liberty,
> As when the war-trump of the wind
> Upstirs our dark blue sea.
>
> His arm was in the foremost rank,

Where enbattled thousands roll
His name was in the love of Greece,
And his spell was on her soul!
   ('Stanzas', 21-28)

The theme was consistent: in her later work Byron has been over-taken by her other hero, Napoleon, commemorated in 'Crowned and Buried'. She had watched Napoleon's exile on Elba and had indignantly compared him in her notebook to Prometheus — 'The heart of the modern Prometheus was exposed to the vultures; but though daily devoured, never became less great'. 'Crowned and Buried' was occasioned by the return of Napoleon's ashes to France in 1840, when the 'lone ship' carrying them had rested at Torquay, the scene of Elizabeth's convalescence.

Later still her hero was Louis Napoleon, whom she saw as a possible saviour. He would free Italy from the constraints of Austrian rule as Byron had championed the struggle of Greece against the Turks. This was a prime purpose of poetry: to direct attention to and influence the events and issues of the time, and Elizabeth Barrett was proud to join Byron in this end. Her last volume, published after her death, and *Poems Before Congress*, maintain the theme to the end. *Poems Before Congress* 'written,' as she describes them in the Preface, 'under the pressure of the events they indicate' (Italian liberation and unification), are full of her indignation at the plight of Italy in its struggle against oppressors — and she writes 'simply because I love both truth and justice *quand même*' (Preface). The first poem is a hymn of praise to the greatness of the deliverer (as she saw him), Napoleon III:

... he might have had the world with him,
But chose to side with suffering men,
And had the world against him when
He came to deliver Italy.
   Emperor
    Evermore.
   ('Napoleon III in Italy', 413-418)

These poems are directly political, and reflect Elizabeth Barrett's passion for politics, which had grown and flourished in the congenial atmosphere of Hope End. Her absorption from the first in the lives and fortunes of nations across the Channel marks her as

101

a remarkable and early European. Even her diary is scattered with references to contemporary foreign affairs seen from Herefordshire (her friend's arrival 'put all my good resolutions [to read Greek] to the route — as the Dutch have lately done the Belgians' [*Diary*, 9, 75]). But her political concern, deep though it was, was not greater than her social concern. As she put it herself in the Preface to *Poems Before Congress*:

> ... non-intervention in the affairs of neighbouring states is a high political virtue; but non-intervention does not mean passing by on the other side when your neighbour falls among thieves ...

and her own preoccupations in politics are as much with individuals as issues. 'The Cry of the Children' is a central poem in her important *Poems* (1844), and was prompted by the report on child labour written by her friend R.H. Horne. It would be easy to dismiss the poem with embarrassment perhaps, for what we might term its sentimentality, but the images of the children toiling like slaves in the factories and mines of newly-urban England —

> 'For oh,' say the children, 'we are weary,
> And we cannot run or leap:
> If we cared for any meadows, it were merely
> To drop down in them and sleep ...
> For, all day, we drag our burden tiring
> Through the coal — dark underground;
> Or, all day, we drive the wheels of iron
> In the factories, round and round.'
> ('The Cry of the Children', 65-68, 73-76)

— conveyed the problems of the society created by the Industrial Revolution more vividly than anything Horne could write, and influenced a wider section of the community.

Among her very last poems is 'A Song for the Ragged Schools of London' (her sister Arabel was much involved in the movement). It is an indignant cry to the 'lordly English' that the pride, wealth, and power of England and her empire are based on foundations of cruelty: the wealth of the newly-rich middle classes — 'Princes' parks and merchants' homes' — is built on 'ruins worse than Rome's,/In your pauper men and women':

Women leering through the gas
(Just such bosoms used to move you),
Men, turned wolves by famine, — pass!
These can speak themselves, and curse you.

But those others — children small,
Spilt like blots about the city,
Quay, and street, and palace wall
Take them up into your pity! ...

Ragged children, hungry-eyed,
Huddled up out of the coldness
On your doorsteps, side by side,
Till your footman damns their boldness.
       ('A Song for the Ragged Schools of London', 41-48, 53-56)

The paradox of the 'nation's empery ... asserted by starvation' is poignantly encapsulated in the wronged, sickly, ragged children who 'spot our streets', the 'scurf and mildew of the city' — a political lesson which the rich must note and learn from before it is too late.

Similarly 'The Runaway Slave at Pilgrim's Point', a central poem in *Poems* (1850): Elizabeth Barrett's horror at the slave system (still in operation in the southern states of America, though abolished in the British Empire) is expressed in the words of the individual slave, a woman who has been raped by her white master. She kills her new-born child ('... the babe who lay on my bosom so, /Was too white, too white for me!') because

I saw a look that made me mad!
The master's look, that used to fall
On my soul like his lash ... or worse!
       ('The Runaway Slave at Pilgrim's Point', 115-116, 143-145)

Slavery was a political issue that came home to Elizabeth Barrett most forcefully — she was to write ruefully to Ruskin in 1855, 'I belong to a family of West Indian slaveholders' (L., II, 220). At home, when she was a young woman, the news from overseas which most concerned her and her family was the fortunes of the slave trade. Though the family prosperity depended directly on what happened to the sugar trade, all the Barretts were abolitionists. Edward Barrett had been born in the West Indies on the family plantation, and knew from an impressionable age the horrors of the slave system.

He always felt concern for the slaves (in 1807 he was arranging for clothes to be sent to them from England), and in the period preceding Abolition he was writing seriously to the legal authorities in Jamaica about social conditions in the plantations. (His tutor, a father-figure in the years he had spent at Trinity College, Cambridge, had also been an active campaigner against slavery.) The faltering fortunes of the Barrett plantation, though more directly connected with the lawsuit which was to devastate it financially, were still uneasily implicated in the growing tension with the slaves, and Elizabeth Barrett has more than one reference to the insurrections that flared up on or near their property in the run-up to Abolition. She was to write to Anna Jameson later, 'You think a woman has no business with questions like the question of slavery? Then she had better use a pen no more. She had better subside into slavery and concubinage herself' (L, II, 110-111).

Equal with politics was religion. Religion had an importance in Elizabeth Barrett's life which may be difficult for some modern readers to understand. She belonged to no particular church but, at least for all the time she lived in England, attended many. All the significant rites of passage — baptism, marriage, burial — were marked by the observances of the Church of England, but her inward religion was a private thing, and intense. Her writing throughout her time at Hope End and later in London — her letters, her diary, her autobiographical essays — testifies to the significance of religion in her life. She was baptised in the parish church near Durham, the county of her birth, but no evidence has come to light that her membership of the church was ever ratified by confirmation, and she wrote to a correspondent much later, 'I am not myself a member of the C of E ... I believe that I do not sin against [the Church of Christ] schismatically as long as I love Christ and recognise in Him the brotherhood of all Believers. As there are many mansions in Heaven, so are there many Churches on earth ...' (Letter to William Merry, in *The Religious Opinions of Elizabeth Barrett Browning*, 34).

From infancy she was brought up in a remarkable spirit of ecumenism. A family from the social class of the Barretts might have been expected automatically to view themselves as an integral part of the national church; but her father, though he was a deep and serious Christian, always remained detached from the parish church, and was on cool terms with the vicar, though he was a frequent attender at St James, Colwall, and most of his children were baptised there. Churchgoing was an important part of the routine at Hope End, and weekly attendance at church, of whatever denomination, was a duty Edward Barrett required from all the family. One of Elizabeth's few altercations with 'Bummy' was over her reluctance to go to St James: 'Feeling convinced as I do that the gospel is not consistently preached there, and that my time can be more usefully and scripturally occupied at home, am I right in going? I think not; but there was so much thunder and lightning about it that I yielded the point' (*Diary*, 124). The sacramental side of religion, and the outward forms and signs, interested Elizabeth not at all, and she was as regularly present in the congregation of the Baptist minister, George Curzon, of Ledbury, as at St James, frequently on the same day, as was her father. Even in the days before the Oxford reformers of 1833, she found the rubrics and language of the Prayer Book quite unnecessarily opaque: she wrote heatedly in her diary, 'I wish the sacramental service were shortened, and weeded of its expressions "holy mysteries", etc. What mystery is there, can there be, in this simple rite?' (*Diary*, 139) though she took the sacrament at St James whenever it was celebrated.

The time of Elizabeth Barrett's girlhood and adolescence in the early decades of the century is traditionally accounted a period of some torpor and stagnation in the Church of England, and the corner of Herefordshire in which she lived gives ample testimony of it. In a great number of parishes the eucharist was celebrated only three times in the year, and the rubrics concerning the other rites and observances of the church were largely disregarded. Preaching had sometimes assumed an importance that dismayed later reformers. In Colwall, certainly, Sacrament Sunday happened three times in the year, and the focal point of the weekly service was the pulpit. Edward Barrett was an earnest Low Churchman, and he and his eldest daughter were expert in assessing the quality of the sermon, to whichever congregation it was delivered. Mr Curzon preached to a Baptist gathering every week in the chapel near the gate at Hope End, and the Barretts would appraise him critically, usually finding him much more 'heartwarming' than Mr Dean, who had preached at Morning Service at St James, though even Mr Curzon often failed to meet their high standards.

In the Regency period, and throughout Elizabeth Barrett's childhood and youth, the Hope End parish of Colwall, then, was a pattern of the low morale of the Anglican church. It was in the gift of the

Bishop of Hereford, George Isaac Huntingford (1815-32), who was himself part of the pattern. He was a rank pluralist who enjoyed the revenues of the see but lived in Winchester where he was Warden. He had presented the parish, we learn from an indignant letter to *The Times*, to a disreputable relative, a non-resident who lived 'in a state of beggary, drunkenness and infamy', and was the nominal curate of various surrounding parishes, but could attend to his priestly functions in any of them only 'when sufficiently sober' (*Diary*, 289). When Elizabeth was twenty-two the parishioners of Colwall had with difficulty obtained the removal of this incumbent and secured the appointment of Mr Dean, who, by contrast, 'diligently fulfilled all the duties of a parish priest', visited the sick, relieved the poor, and conducted services twice every Sunday (*Diary*, 289). But even as Elizabeth was writing her diary at the end of 1831 the fortunes of the Colwall parish foundered: the letter to *The Times* complained bitterly to the bishop

> Upon the recent death of our long absent rector [the bishop's kinsman], a petition was immediately forwarded to your Lordship from the inhabitants and landowners of this parish, requesting you to appoint our curate [Mr Clark] to the living ... The only result ... has been the appointment of a stranger, a pluralist who has no intention of residing, and is about to remove our worthy curate to make way for a young relative preparing for orders.
> (*Diary*, 289-90)

One corner of Herefordshire stepped back into the Regency world. Elizabeth, who had little inherent affection for the national church and less for its dignitaries, expressed no strong feelings on the situation, though she commended her friend Mr Martin a shade ironically for the severity of his letter in *The Times* ('He will have the whole church militant in this part of the world upon him!' [*Diary*, 290]) and deplored that he wrote as a magistrate rather than a theologian. She herself was impatient with what she saw as the wilful obscurantism of the church, and her view of Mr Clark fell short of the case made for him in *The Times*. She would judge an individual on his merits and was sceptical of organised religion in any form.

The coming changes in the Anglican church she predictably viewed with a shudder. The growing emphasis on the sacramental and the insistence on a closer reading of the rubrics of the Prayer Book, ran counter to what she saw as the 'simpler form of worship and teaching' which she professed 'by temperament and affection'. The Roman Catholic church she viewed with out-and-out horror, and the 'Puseyites' as simply schismatic. It was a part of the case against Henrietta's subsequent suitor, Lieutenant Surtees Cook, that he espoused Tractarian views. Elizabeth, though, always felt more tolerance towards individuals than systems and was to later write to her sister lovingly of Surtees' 'ecclesiastical reproofs, which I should always take as *proofs* of his brotherly love' (LS, 301). To her father, however, Cook's High Churchism lent justification to his prejudice against the marriage. Elizabeth's own views always emphasised the universality of religion. 'Christ's church,' after all, 'is one. My creed is that controversy does harm,' she wrote to a correspondent in 1841. When her own son was born nearly twenty years after the Barretts left Hope End, he was baptised not at the English church in Florence but at the French Lutheran church, with no ceremony at all; and friends in Florence like Mrs David Ogilvy thought of both the Brownings as 'keen Dissenters' (LMDO, xxvii).

In Hope End days the most dear and familiar religion was in the household prayers read by her father or later by Bro, his eldest son, to the assembled family. They followed no form and were based on scripture: Elizabeth studies the texts regularly ('Read, as I do every day, seven chapters of Scripture', [*Diary*, 19]) and corresponded earnestly with Mr Boyd on biblical subjects. Sundays were almost exclusively times of some kind of organised religion ('Driving to church — driving back again — driving to chapel — driving back again — and prayers three times at home besides! All that fills up the day — except the few interstices between the intersections' [*Diary*, 5]). The clergyman who ministered to them weekly in the chapel at the gate was the Honourable and Reverend George Curzon, who preached on scriptural doctrine — on prayer and faith, far from controversy. Mr Clark, who preached at St James, Colwall, was a Low Churchman, to whom Elizabeth listened critically. Sundays in fact were kept rigorously. Birthdays were holidays in the Barrett family, but should they fall on a Sunday, all celebrations were deferred: 'not kept, but thought of' (*Diary*, 33).

From childhood, religion was clearly a central preoccupation, and more and more not to be separated from the prime preoccupation of her life, poetry. 'At twelve', she recorded solemnly in *Glimpses Into My*

Own Life, 'I was in great danger of becoming the founder of a religion of my own. I revolted at the idea of an established religion — my faith was sincere, but my religion was founded solely on the imagination.'

> So great was the strength of my imagination, which is now often too powerful for my control. This year [1818] I read Milton for the first time *thro* together with Shakespeare and Pope's Homer ...
> (Autobiographical Essays, 352)

The climax of this intense mental activity came in this year with her completion of *The Battle of Marathon*: her religious life and her imaginative life had a common source. From fourteen she looked back at this happy period as one of exaltation, when contemplation of 'enthusiastic visions' led her first to poetry and then to God. In her maturer years she is less ardent but more reasonable. With the publication of *The Battle of Marathon* in 1820 'My religious enthusiasm had subsided, and I took upon myself to advocate the cause of the Church of England! This was a curious change but I was borne away from all reason by the power, the fatal power, of my imagination' (ibid.).

It is predictable, in the circumstances, that from the beginning so much of Elizabeth Barrett's poetry should be religious. In an age that was so conscious of religion, and so tormented by religious questions, it was a topic that occupied most imaginative writers at some level. (Elizabeth Barrett herself said 'An irreligious poet is no poet at all', for 'the gravitation of poetry is upwards'.) The finest of such poetry is the anguished expression of doubt (famously Tennyson's in *In Memoriam*, and in the plangency of Arnold's *Scholar-Gypsy*) and the struggle for faith of Hopkins. But throughout the century there was a line of devotional poets such as Keble, Isaac Williams and Christina Rossetti in which Elizabeth Barrett makes an honourable appearance. She does not attempt to embrace the great religious questions of the day, or confront the dilemmas posed by Darwin and Chambers and the biblical critics, but expresses a quiet traditional faith untroubled by the *angst* of the contemporary church in the face of the discoveries of geology and palaeontology. For her the relationship of the soul with its Maker is based on confidence in the Redeemer and calm acceptance of God's will and love. In 'Idols' in her earliest work, for instance, she vows to worship not her former idols, Beauty, Love, and Fame ('for three times they betrayed me') but God who comprehends them all, 'Who deathless love in death declarest / None else is beauteous — famous — dear!'. The series of Hymns, published with other poems, in *The Seraphim* ('A Supplication for Love', 'The Mediator', 'The Weeping Saviour', 'The Measure') stress the Atonement, the loving kindness of the Victim and His accessibility to a fallen race:

> High God, and pure, and strong, and kind!
> The low, the foul, the feeble, spare!
> The brightness in His face we find
> Behold our darkness only there!
> ('The Mediator', 17-20)

More ambitiously, in her Preface to *The Seraphim* (1838), she discusses her intention to write poems 'religious in their general character', which demonstrate the love of God in the atonement of Christ through the Crucifixion — 'By this and this only can we know it — that Christ laid down His life for us'. She presents in a 'dramatic lyric' contrasting views of the Crucifixion through the eyes of two angels, and concludes triumphantly with her conviction that the Saviour has assured 'that the weak, like me, before / His heavenly throne should walk in white' (*The Seraphim*, 1050-1051).

Elizabeth's conservative, even conventional, faith remained unchallenged by the Victorian spectres of the mind. Rather less conventional, though it was of its time, was her notorious enthusiasm for spiritualism, a form of faith she found no difficulty in reconciling with Christianity. She was particularly anxious to be reassured on questions of the resurrection of the body and personal immortality as more and more of those in her life passed over to the other side — her mother first, then Bro, and then later her father and her sister Henrietta — and was eager for these manifestations from the afterlife. She encountered the vogue in Florence and fell for it headlong to the embarrassed dismay of her husband Robert, who wrote 'Mr Sludge the Medium'. Elizabeth was undeterred. Though it threatened to be the most serious disagreement she had with her husband, this could not check her obsession. She had been interested in the supernatural long before she met Robert. The marvels of mesmerism had thrilled and awed her when she was in Wimpole Street in the 1840s, she had read with absorption the works of Swedenborg, the mystic and visionary who seemed to be in direct contact with the spiritual world, and even at Hope End she had been anxious to believe the ghost stories told in the servants' hall. The ground was well prepared for the experiences of table-rapping and communion with spirits which she encountered in the drawing-rooms of Florence.

Robert was appalled that a woman of his wife's critical intelligence should be so engrossed by the 'twaddle' of spiritualism, not acknowledging it as another manifestation of her religious life. But to Elizabeth the surge in the popularity of spiritualism was a welcome sign, an obvious challenge to the rampant materialism and infidelity of the age, and a reaffirmation of spiritual values in the face of the utilitarian ethos of the time. Her poetry, both political and religious, had always celebrated such values. The heroes of her political poetry, Byron and both the Napoleons, were representatives to her of super-human ideals, and her 'social' poetry, even before her masterpiece *Aurora Leigh*, established and demonstrated her belief in things outside the material. Though the rites and customs of spiritualism seemed simply absurd to Robert, and its practitioners ridiculous, to her and to many serious and notable people it was wholly acceptable.

Of all the themes of poets, love is perhaps the most recurrent. It is normal for clever and articulate girls (Elizabeth was both) to create a fully-detailed alter ego with whom they can identify, and Elizabeth created 'Beth', whom she describes for her young cousin. 'Beth', the tomboy, the despiser of all things 'feminine', the poet, the warrior who will deliver Greece from Turkish rule, has another passionate characteristic, her 'love of life' and her determination to be loved. For 'Beth'/Elizabeth, the lover will come when she reaches the unimaginable age of fifteen — though he will be an undemanding lover, content to be 'in love' without the restrictions implied by marriage.

The question of 'love', whether familial, social or sexual, is one at the back of Elizabeth's mind throughout the time she was growing up. Although like 'Beth' she is her own person ('My love of solitude is growing with my growth', she notes in her diary, 'I am inclined to shun the acquaintance of those whom I do not like and love' [*Diary*, 155]), she is still anxious about the opinion of those whom she does like and love. When she was a child, such people were her family, and her love for them she notes in *Autobiographical Essays*, 'can scarcely be defined'. Her love is general, but in its most particular form it is reserved for Bro, the brother to whom she was closest.

> If I ever loved any human being I love this dear Brother ... the
> partner of my pleasures of my literary toils. My attachment
> to him is literally devoted! If to save him from anxiety ... any
> effort of mine could suffice, Heaven knows my heart that I
> would unhesitatingly buy his happiness with my own misery!
>   (*Autobiographical Essays*, 354)

She had been much put out as a child to be told by an aggrieved
servant girl that she was 'cold and unfeeling, and that everyone
thought so, whatever they might say' (*Autobiographical Essays*, 349),
but the feelings she expressed for Bro suggest quite the contrary. Her
feelings for her father, at least in these early years, were summed up
in a birthday poem from her adolescence:

> No thoughts of fondness e'er appear
> More fond, than those I write of here!
> No name can e'er on tablet shine,
> My father! more belov'd than thine!
>   ('To my Father on his Birthday', 9-12)

and her anguish on the death of her mother in 1828 is transcribed in
her letters.

Until she was a young woman her relationships within the family
were the deepest ones she experienced, and convention permitted
her to articulate them. She could own that her attachment there was
'a sentiment at once sincere, enthusiastic, devoted' and feel that any
life outside these confines was intolerable to think of. The love she
wrote of in her earliest verse, before she was twenty, was the safely
distant love of Riego's widow for her husband, the long-dead martyr
to the Spanish cause ('On a Picture of Riego's Widow'), as much a
celebration of the cause as of the man; or her love for Bro in 'Verses
for my Brother', or Bro's for her in the recollections of 'Memory'. The
first serious relationship outside her family, with Hugh Boyd, is
recorded in her (too brief) diary, and even there the depth of her
feelings must be to some extent inferred. But she grows almost
visibly older under the strength of the attachment she can barely
understand and does not yet know how to handle. The whole
question of love is one she can scarcely articulate in this context, even
in a diary, that most confidential of media, and its pages are full of
half-expressed thoughts on love in general and Hugh Boyd in particular. Her greatest fear is that he does not recognise, or repudiates,

her love. 'I wish I were more sure of his regard,' she sighs, '... If he cared for me as I care for him, he would speak and act only in one way' (*Diary*, 17). 'It is painful to be *longing* to love a person who will not be loved or to *love* a person who repays your love with such coldness — such unkindness!' (*Diary*, 2). It has ever been her lot in life, she mourns, to find affection least where she desires it most, and to provoke it where she cares least ('I wonder why they all like me so much at Ruby Cottage — I mean, why Miss Boyd and Miss Gibbons and Miss Bordman like me so much. It is always so! — I am liked most by those whom — but such reflections are "vainest of all vain things"' [*Diary*, 128]). An affectionate gesture, she persuades herself, is all she looks for ('An affectionate manner certainly does go to my heart which is itself far too affectionate!' [*Diary*, 124]) and she is satisfied with so little. But as it is she can only exclaim on the pangs of love: 'Oh, the pain attendant on liking and loving, may seem a little cloud — but it blots from us all the light of the sun!!' (*Diary*, 155).

The relationship with Boyd was the most important thing in her life in the last five years she was at Hope End, and her poems from 1826 and throughout the 1830s contain themes of this love — love despised, love rejected, love betrayed. The central character in 'The Romance of Margaret', for instance, sings of the failure of love: the spirit who comes to Margaret tells her that all the relationships in her life most dear to her — with her brother, with her little sister, with her old father, with the Knight she loves — are all over, that 'love is transient too,' and Margaret, in despair, ends her own life. What she has invested in relationships, in fact, has brought her no returns — she has no identity outside them, and as they fail she can only embrace the nothingness of death. It is a powerful poem of loss which says much of Elizabeth Barrett's state of mind in the period after Hugh Boyd.

The victim in 'A Romance of the Ganges', another ballad in the same volume, is again a woman, Luti, betrayed by her lover, who has taken another bride. As she sits weeping by the Ganges, Luti reflects that her love seems twice betrayed. Almost simultaneously death has taken her father and treachery her bridegroom. Her resentment spreads like miasma to infect the joy of her successful rival Nuleeni, as she sits watching the little lighted boat, the symbol of her happiness, as it floats down the Ganges on her bridal day. The pain attendant on liking and loving, in fact, lingers in the poet's mind, and while the little boat floats on, Luti 'weepeth dark with sorrow' ('A Romance of the Ganges', 212).

Love of other kinds in the volume is no less equivocal. 'Isobel's Child', for instance, takes an image of great poignancy in a mother and her dying child, and juxtaposes the passionate prayer of the mother for the child's recovery with the baby's own anguished rejoinder that he feels his mother's love as a curb:

> It bindeth me, it holdeth me,
> With its most loving cruelty.
> ('Isobel's Child', 396-397)

He pleads that he be allowed to die and find freedom in Heaven. Isobel is persuaded and relaxes her hold, tacitly acknowledging the child's argument.

> Love! Earth's love! and *can* we love
> Fixedly where all things move?
> Can the sinning love each other?
> (498-500)

The nurse finds her later with the lifeless child in her arms, and is awed by her resigned acceptance of the child's will. Even in an age which endorsed the convention of a better world awaiting a child as yet undefiled by this one, the mother's unresisting relinquishment of human love, and unquestioning recognition that the child had chosen the better path, must have seemed exaggerated. To the reader of today the poem must say as much of Elizabeth Barrett's brooding on the unreliableness of any love as of her piety.

The time of her childhood and youth at Hope End was one she came to view equivocally in the light of her later experience. She observed in *Sonnets from the Portuguese*:

> I lived with visions for my company
> Instead of men and women, years ago,
> And found them gentle mates, nor thought to know
> A sweeter music than they played to me.
> (26)

On the surface it represented an idyll of security in terms of family love — but the seeds of possible discord were always there, especially with her father.

Of all Elizabeth Barrett's poetry *Sonnets from the Portuguese*, the poems of her own love, have been the most enduringly popular. Any anthology of English poetry is likely to include more from this collection than any other, and in the present *Oxford Book of English Verse*, for example, three of her six poems included are from the sonnets. The line of her verse most familiar to most people (due in part, no doubt, to the greeting card industry) must be 'How do I love thee? Let me count the ways'(43). The sonnets have their roots in Hope End, though they were not published till 1850: the title of the collection is a kind of private joke shared with Browning. For another love-lyric she records in her diary as having written before they left Hope End in 1832 was 'Catarina to Camoens', the lament of Catarina to her lover, the Portuguese hero, to which the later title is a subtle allusion. *Sonnets from the Portuguese* suggests that the poems are translations, and at the same time that they are from the hand of the Portuguese woman of the earlier poem. Both devices direct the reader away from the 'personal' element in the sonnets, and suggest that they should be read as dramatic monologues, that safely-distanced form of identity concealed behind identity popularised by Browning himself. But in fact *Sonnets from the Portuguese* is the only work in which Elizabeth Barrett directly tells her own story.

The story is familiar, and part of the myth of the most famous of literary elopements. Elizabeth Barrett wrote the sonnets during Robert Browning's year of covert courtship, between the day when he succeeded in crossing the threshold of 50 Wimpole Street in May 1845 and the September afternoon in 1846 when they left it together for Italy. Browning knew nothing of them until she laid them before him in September 1849: forty-four sonnets detailing through her eyes the whole course of their love, from its hesitant beginning, when she could hardly bring herself to believe that the love he offered was true, and the weeks that followed of doubt and misgiving, to the joyful acceptance that their love was mutual. Sidney, Spenser and Shakespeare had written sonnet sequences in the Renaissance which narrated the story of a love, but always in the conventional mode, and from the point of view of the active partner, the man, who laid claim to the woman, the object of his desire, and won her with a conscious strategy. Elizabeth Barrett, in resurrecting the sonnet sequence, spoke with a different voice, the voice of the woman who was also the poet. Novel again, it is the poet wooing the poet, for they are both artists, and neither occupies a customary role: the woman is not the passive recipient of male desire, expressed through the male prerogative of poetry, and the object addressed is not conventionally wooed and won by strategy, but an equal. It is a paradoxical situation, not so much a simple reversal of roles as a startling redistribution of conventional elements; for the woman, anxious to be won, is nevertheless assuming the active role in addressing the man, and speaking to him as one poet to another. The popularity of the sonnets has always been due as much to their 'truth' and their 'sincerity' — the same 'personal' qualities which Browning had most disliked in poetry, and had sought to avoid with the dramatic monologue — as to the new direction they mark in her poetry. The story begins with the voice of the habitual invalid who has been surprised by joy: 'Guess now who holds thee', says a figure who grasps her by the hair.

> 'Death' I said. But there,
> The silver answer rang — 'Not Death, but Love'
>   (1)

She is startled at the unlooked-for visitor, having expected to stand on 'the dreadful outer brink of obvious death' (7) sooner than on the 'dewless asphodel' (27) of earthly happiness. She questions in sonnet after sonnet if she is worthy of the love. She deplores her age, her seeming ingratitude, the paucity of the gifts she brings to him, she urges that he repeat his vows of love over and over again, and she preserves his every letter as further proof of his vow. Then as confidence and trust grow ('I lean upon thee, Dear, without alarm,/And feel as safe as guarded by a charm', [24]) she gives him a lock of hair in return for his, and begs him to call her by her pet-name, as her mother did. She wonders wistfully about the pang of leaving home and everything dear to her ('Home-talk and blessing and the common kiss /That comes to each in turn', [35]). But there is no real hesitation as she reflects on the nature of the exchange expressed in the physical demonstrations of his love:

> First time he kissed me, he but only kissed
> The fingers of this hand wherewith I write;
> And ever since it grew more clean and white,
> Slow to world-greetings, quick with its 'Oh, list,'
> When the angels speak. A ring of amethyst

I could not wear here, plainer to my sight,
Than that first kiss. The second passed in height
The first, and sought the forehead, and half missed,
Half falling on the hair. O beyond meed!
That was the chrism of love, which love's own crown,
With sanctifying sweetness, did precede.
The third upon my lips was folded down
In perfect, purple state; since when, indeed,
I have been proud and said, 'My love, my own'.
    (38)

After the third kiss, on the lips, any misgivings on the change she
purposes vanish in the conviction that this sublimer love she shares
with her lover has surpassed anything 'called love, forsooth' (40).
The tone of the final sonnets is strong and confident, and they
conclude with the emblem of the flowers he has brought the year
round to 'this close room' in Wimpole Street, which now signify his
love rooted for ever in her heart:

Beloved, thou hast brought me many flowers
Plucked in the garden, all the summer through
And winter, and it seemed as if they grew
In this close room, nor missed the sun and showers.
So, in the like name of that love of ours ...
Instruct thine eyes to keep their colours true,
And tell thy soul their roots are left in mine.
    (44)

Seven:
1846-1861: Life in Italy

This book has been centred on the crucial early years of Elizabeth Barrett Browning's life in Herefordshire, crucial both in themselves and in their influence on her later life. The last fifteen years of her life were of course spent very far from Herefordshire, in Italy. Even there she never forgot her childhood.

After the secret marriage and elopement the Brownings left for their new life in Italy on 19 September 1846. Italy, so long denied her by her father, was to be the place, they reasoned, where Elizabeth would find health. Their destination when they left was Pisa, and there for some few months they made their first home together, and there in March 1847 Elizabeth suffered her first miscarriage. Then in April that year they moved on to Florence, which as well as being more attractive, was cheaper, and in July they established themselves at the address which was to be their home (with short breaks) for the rest of their life together, Casa Guidi. Here was the site for the major events of her later life, both professional and personal.

In terms of her literary career the best was still to come. First came the publication in England of the poems which confirmed her popular reputation, already established by the *Poems* of 1844, the collection of *Poems* of 1850. It contained the poems on Hugh Boyd, and such popular poems as 'The Runaway Slave at Pilgrim's Point' and 'Hector in the Garden'. It was also the time of the sonnets published as *Sonnets from the Portuguese*, the forty-four Petrachan sonnets in which she writes directly of her own experience in a series of tightly-wrought poems of psychological analysis linked with a strong narrative line. Then from her experience in Italy came two volumes of political poetry (politics had always been her passion), *Casa Guidi Windows* (1851) and *Poems Before Congress* (1860). It was a critical period in the political history of Italy, and almost from the moment of arrival Elizabeth Barrett Browning was passionately involved with the issues in debate. Between the two volumes came her 'novel in verse' *Aurora Leigh*, written in Florence and Paris, which is her masterpiece (1856) and was received as such by her contemporaries. She had always felt that the best poetry was written under pressure and was created out of suffering. Now experience proved her wrong. She and Browning had discussed endlessly the work they would do in their future together, and when the honeymoon period was over and the settled happiness of life together in the gentler airs of Italy became a routine, she began her best work.

But Casa Guidi was the locale for the triumphs of her personal life too. In early 1848 she knew she was pregnant again, but in March she had a second miscarriage. Her third pregnancy, however, was successful. On 9 March 1849, three days after her forty-third birthday, was born Robert Wiedman Browning, called 'Pen'. Elizabeth's pride in this achievement was quite as great as in anything else she accomplished: she, known everywhere as the invalid of Wimpole Street, had produced, in middle-age and with minimum trouble, a triumphantly perfect baby. She boasted to Miss Mitford of the doctor's opinion 'that in all his practice he had never seen the functions of nature more healthfully performed', and to her sister Henrietta she confided that Robert had said 'I feel as if I could give my life for him already'. They named him Wiedman (after Robert's mother, who died within days of the baby's birth), but he called himself 'Penini', in a vain attempt to master the syllables, and so he remained.

Pen was the object of both his parents' unfailing, unqualified adoration. The summer before Pen's birth another English couple, Mr and Mrs David Ogilvy, had taken up residence in Florence, and through a Barrett cousin had met and liked the Brownings; and their son Alexander was born there in September, six months before Pen. The following October the Ogilvys moved to the apartment above the Brownings in Casa Guidi, and the two mothers became firm friends. The two families spent several summers together in Bagni di Lucca, Venice, and one in Paris, and even met in London, first for the Great Exhibition in 1851, and then on various other occasions.

The fullest and most numerous accounts of Pen's early years are to be found in the letters from Elizabeth to her friend when they are apart. The friendship between the mothers lasted until Elizabeth

Barrett Browning's death in 1861, when Pen was twelve. The baby's amazing precocity in terms of his weight, his rosiness, his teeth, his bright eyes, his liveliness, and his intelligence are an important part of every letter, with an enquiry at the end of the eulogy about the similar progress of Alexander and sometimes of Mrs Ogilvy's other children.

As Pen and Alexander get older the exchanges between the anxious mothers concern upbringing and education. The Browning parents had as many principles about what children should be taught as the Barretts ever had, but these are different, at least as regards their own child. The Barretts, though flexible and imaginative in their attitude by the standards of the time, still followed the rules of convention in the tutors and governesses they employed for their children from an early age (Elizabeth remained in touch with Mrs Orme to the end, and was visiting her in London in 1856). But the Brownings agreed that Pen, the fairy child, was not to touch the bloom of his innocence with knowledge until the proper time; 'the fairies', his mother told Henrietta, 'forbid it'. 'I must confess to you', she said when Pen was four,

> I am teaching him to read. I want him to know how to read for his own pleasure's sake and that he may inherit the fat of fairyland, and not that I have the least notion of beginning a course of education.
> (LS, 14 May 1853)

He was to do his important growing up without the restraints of formal teaching, and for as long as he would, simply absorbing the art and music and culture which were the civilization of Italy. Pen, though he was in no hurry to enter the prison house of conventional learning, submitted to other disciplines quite willingly. Robert gave him piano lessons every day, and from early childhood he was very good at drawing.

Elizabeth was particularly fierce, strangely enough, about teaching him Latin and Greek, the normal rite of passage for any English boy of his age and class (she said it was because of the Italian pronunciation of the vowels — shades of Uvedale Price!), and was much in sympathy with the theory expressed by some educationists that a child should learn the living languages first and the dead languages later.

So Pen did not begin Latin, or anything else, until he was eleven.

The Brownings spent the winter of 1860 in Rome, when a young abbé came — almost casually — to begin Pen's education in the conventional disciplines, Latin, French, arithmetic and geography. 'You may imagine Pen's innocence as to figures when I tell you [Mrs Ogilvy] that before we went to Rome he never could be 'quite sure', he said, 'which was a 6 and which a 9, as to the tails going up or down', (LMDO, 15 June 1860). All the same, he spoke and wrote Italian and English interchangeably, and would read French and German with his mother, though his spelling in all of them was always one of his 'weak points' (LMDO, 30 January 1859).

Pen was dressed (in his mother's lifetime, anyway) in an effeminate style that startled the Italians, and at nine was still wearing lace collars, embroidered short trousers, and high blouses of velvet or merino, and his hair still flowed in curls — 'a long sweep of golden brown ringlets' (LMDO, 6 March 1855). Elizabeth Barrett was horrified to hear that Alexander Ogilvy (with regulation short hair) and Henrietta's son Altham were to be sent to school, for nothing would ever persuade her to part with Pen. There was never any question of it, of course, during his mother's lifetime, in spite of her brothers' standard education at Charterhouse and Robert, himself home educated, raised no apparent demur. It seems strange, in view of Elizabeth's own longing for a formal education, and her fierce envy of Bro's opportunities at Charterhouse, that she should have felt so little of such anxiety on Pen's behalf. Robert would have been glad to send him to the upper forms of a public school later, to prepare him for the university, but never did. In spite of this Elizabeth did to an extent relive her own childhood in her letters about Pen. Like her, he proved remarkably good at languages, he was as passionate and partisan about politics as she had always been, he sporadically devoured novels with her enthusiasm ('O Dumas, Dumas, you ARE a great man! to write a book [*Monte Cristo*] magnificent like this!' [LMDO, 30 January 1859]), he rode a pony much like Moses, and she was as reluctant to let him grow up as her own parents had been.

His formative years, in fact, were largely undisciplined ('Once ... he has been punished. Robert punished him, much to my disapprobation, for I disapprove of hard-hearted people ...' [LMDO, 9 September 1853]), and Pen paid the price. He never shared his mother's scholarly bent, as she acknowledged wistfully, and though after her death his father did his best ('I shall give myself up to the care and education of our child; I know all Ba's mind on how that should be, and shall try to carry out her desires' [LGB, 2 July 1861]), old habits were too strong, and Pen never did anything academically. Subsequently he spent some time at Christ Church, where he enjoyed himself thoroughly, but left without a degree. His father conceded ruefully that he was 'unfit for anything but idleness and pleasure' (LGB, 1 July 1870).

One thing Pen could do, however, was paint. His childish talent for drawing matured into real artistic ability, and his mother encouraged this and his music enthusiastically. Before he was four he was presenting his pictures to his parents' friends, Ruskin and Millais, and when he decided to make art his career (though he would have preferred to be a cavalry officer) Millais was most encouraging, and 'said all we could hope or wish' about his pictures. After his unpromising beginnings in other lines, his father was delighted to be able to make report to George Barrett some time later of Pen's 'first success ... One of his pictures is at the Academy, another at the Grosvenor', and to quote the sale of Pen's portrait of himself (LGB, 2 May 1882). Millais saw to it that he studied painting in Antwerp and sculpture in Paris under Rodin. He made a successful career, was recognised everywhere as a good artist, and in the fullness of time returned to Italy. He married an American heiress there in 1887, and bought the Palazzo Rezzonico in Venice. But his marriage was no more successful than his university career, and lasted no longer, though if blame is to be apportioned it seems that Fannie Coddington was the partner who abandoned the marriage. Browning died in Venice in 1889 while on a visit to his son and daughter-in-law.

Pen never met his grandfather. To the end Edward Barrett's anger and resentment remained implacable, and he never saw or communicated with his beloved daughter save once after his initial letter. On her side Elizabeth had hoped for a reconciliation to the end, and had written to him regularly and frequently chronicling the events of her life. On the first visit to London, in the summer of 1851, they had lodged only a short distance from Wimpole Street, and she made many visits there for the joy of being with her sisters, and for a full reconciliation with her brothers. Robert wrote to her father urging with touching humility a healing of old wounds, and Elizabeth wrote again in London begging forgiveness after the five years' penance. Edward Barrett ignored her letter, wrote coldly to Robert, and returned at the same time every letter sent from Italy unopened. It was a cruelty which left his daughter devastated. Then on a later stay in London Pen visited Wimpole Street alone, happy in the care of his Aunt Arabel, and was romping gleefully in the hall with his 'untle' George when the head of the house appeared and gazed at him 'for two or three minutes' — the image, it is said, of Bro at that age — saying nothing. Later he asked, 'Whose child is that?' but on being told made no reply. It was the closest acquaintance ever made between the generations. Edward Barrett made sure that his family was out of town as soon as he knew of the Brownings' visits to London, and though Elizabeth contrived once to follow them to Ventnor, and to visit Henrietta in Somerset, the chances of any meeting between Pen and his grandfather were remote.

One letter he did send his daughter, in September 1852, while they were in London for the second time. This letter has never been traced. It caused her almost the same pain as his silence, seeming to confirm what she had never really believed, that he no longer loved her. It was cold and merciless, she told Henrietta, 'written after six years with the plain intention of giving me as much pain as possible'. We can infer from what she told Henrietta that, far from forgiveness, it was a call for repentance for her sin in failing to 'sacrifice [her] life and its affections' exclusively to him. Elizabeth had written to him as on the previous visit, almost beside herself for a sign of his appeasement, and desperate that a letter might pave the way to a meeting: she knew that Edward Barrett was aware of her presence in London, and was anxious to give him every chance to approach her in any way he chose. But the letter, and its response, merely widened the gap.

Edward Barrett's death occurred unexpectedly in April 1857. The shock to Elizabeth was compounded with the poignancy that a final reconciliation was now impossible. Though he had been no part of her life for nearly twelve eventful years she had never accepted that the breach really was permanent, and had kept his portrait in her room always. She wrote to Henrietta:

> I take up books — but my heart goes walking up and down constantly through that house of Wimpole Street, till it is tired, tired. I dare say it is the same with yours — only you have more children ...
> (LS, 13 May 1857)

She took some brief comfort when she heard of a letter from Mrs Martin in Herefordshire to her father, begging him to forgive his married children. Mr Barrett had replied that 'He had forgiven them, and ... he even prayed for the well-being of their families ... Those were the words', Elizabeth wrote to Henrietta. 'Let us hold them fast. He prayed for us.' But his words were of minimal comfort really, because he never communicated them to his children.

No one will ever know Edward Barrett's own version of the events in his relationship with his eldest daughter, his favourite child. He had always regarded his family, it seems, as somewhat like his Jamaican slaves, and though the Barretts had a reputation for treating their slaves better than most West Indian planters did, this was only relative. The convention on the estate of harshly-enforced authority on one side, and meek, unquestioning obedience on the other was unchallenged. Runaway slaves could still look for flogging, branding, and punishment in the stocks. When Elizabeth, and later Henrietta and Alfred, defied his wishes and married, his instinct born of generations in a West Indian slave culture was of instant repression, and Governor Eyre never acted with swifter brutality. All the children were cut out of his life from that moment and disinherited. His gentle wife, whose background was less directly involved with slaves, and who had never lived on family plantations in Jamaica, was dead, and unable to soften his uncompromising rigour.

This was a worrying and distressing time in Elizabeth Barrett Browning's life. The politics of Italy, with which she identified passionately, were in a state of turbulence at the end of the 1850s, and this was mirrored in her own mind. The nationalistic spirit aroused by the first Napoleon in Italy earlier in the century had led to a surge of patriotism and the idea of the unification of all the Italian States into a single kingdom of Italy. After the Napoleonic Wars the country was divided up among the European powers, with the largest slice going to Austria. Austria ruled Lombardy and Venetia, and the three little duchies of Parma, Modena, and Tuscany were ruled by Austrian princes. The Pope controlled the Papal States and the Bourbons were restored in Naples. Unrest against the occupying powers simmered over the years, particularly against Austria. Plans for unification were hotly discussed on all sides. Elizabeth was an active participant, and had met Mazzini in 1852; but she feared the plans had all come to nothing after the Treaty of Villafranca in July 1859, in which Napoleon III of France, her long time hero, seemed to have sold out to the Austrians and confirmed the Austrian hold on Italy. One of her bitterest poems (in *Poems Before Congress*) is 'A Tale of Villafranca', and a companion poem in *Last Poems* 'First News from Villafranca' rivals it in anguish at the treachery:

> Peace, peace, peace, do you say?
> What! — with the enemy's guns in our ears?
> With the country's wrong not rendered back?
> What! — while Austria stands at bay
> In Mantua, and our Venice bears
> The cursed flag of yellow and black? ...
>
> No, not Napoleon! — he who mused
> At Paris, and at Milan spake,
> And at Solferino led the fight:
> Not he we trusted, honoured, used
> Our hopes and hearts for ... till they break,
> Even so, you tell us ... in his sight.
> ('First News from Villafranca', 1-12)

Her political dreams seemed to be in pieces because of the treachery of her sometime hero Napoleon III at Villafranca, and in her private life too the prospects seemed to be bleak. Her father's death in 1857 was the devastating climax of a series of losses as she heard of the deaths of old friends. Mary Russell Mitford, her earliest friend from the days of Wimpole Street, had died in 1855, and a year later followed the death of possibly the single most significant figure in the Brownings' lives, John Kenyon. From the earliest days of her *Essay on Mind*, when he had written to her in Herefordshire, he had been her staunchest ally. He had acted as friend, benefactor and fairy godmother to them both ever since they met (and he had been behind that too) and was a father figure to Elizabeth throughout her married life. All her letters to every correspondent are full of references to 'Dear Mr Kenyon'. The strongest champion of Browning throughout, he had taken it upon himself to intercede with her father for them when they left England. The 'dearest, best friend to us' had offered them

> A measure uncalled for, unsolicited, unexpected. Sympathy was all we asked for, or thought of receiving, and he gave us head and heart and both warm hands, and thrust himself into most unpleasant positions for a man of his delicacy, rather than lose sight of an interest of mine.
> (LS, 31 March 1847)

He had backed them unreservedly in their decision to marry (he had written 'to applaud to the echo everything we have done'), and more importantly had settled money on them at a time when they needed it most. Once they were abroad, they had spent time with him whenever they could ('Tomorrow we breakfast with Mr Kenyon to meet half America and a quarter of London', [LS, 13 July 1855]. 'We don't leave town on Wednesday ... Mr Kenyon comes to London today, and we are entreated to wait a little, for his sake', [LS, 3 October 1855]). He had always been a centre for literary life in London, and the Brownings had been familiar figures there before their marriage; now they welcomed even more the chance he afforded them to be a part of such congenial company.

They had been with him in his last illness ('Dear Mr Kenyon! Of course we think of very little else' [LS, 7 May, 1856]) when he was at his home in Cowes, and Browning had nursed him there for a time. He had pressed them to use his magnificent and empty house in Devonshire Place, near enough to Wimpole Street, while they were in London, and they had spent several luxurious weeks there, acutely aware of the unaccustomed elegance. His last gesture was his magnificent bequest to them both, which was to leave them both secure and financially independent. But Elizabeth was deeply saddened at his death. She had finished *Aurora Leigh* at his house and dedicated it to him with a moving and heartfelt expression of her obligation:

> [T]hrough my various efforts in literature and steps in Life, you have believed in me, borne with me, and been generous to me, far beyond the common uses of mere relationship or sympathy of mind.

Her own health at this period gave cause for some alarm, and these deaths in her circle may well have had something to contribute. She had enjoyed startlingly good health (for her) in the early years of her marriage, but a winter that they spent in Paris in 1851-1852 saw the real beginning of her decline. She had complained before, it is true, of the climate in London, and the deleterious effect of the air there on her lungs, but the frequency of her reports of her cough, the spitting of blood, breathlessness, and pains in her side, doubles at this juncture. It was a bad winter in Paris, but the summer following was no less trying, and her health hardly improved. They visited

London again, and returned to Florence via Paris late in the autumn, on a journey that ended with Elizabeth's dramatic collapse at Genoa. But the Italian sun shone and her apparent recovery began at once.

The fluctuations in her health continued. The winter of 1854-1855 was bitterly cold for Italy, with snow, frost and a continuing keen wind, and in December 1854 she was visited by 'the worst attack on the chest I have ever suffered from in Italy' (LS, 12 February 1855). The following mild winter in Paris found her 'still not very strong'. She appeared fit again in the summer of 1856, but it did not last and by the winter she was racked permanently with paroxysms of coughing that suggested chronic bronchitis. But still there were long respites between attacks when the baking climate of Italy (in Sienna or Bagni di Lucca when Florence or Rome proved too taxing) worked soothing magic, though after each attack her general condition slipped back a little further.

In the last period of her life the political situation in Italy had an important part to play in the state of her health. She was as emotionally involved in the stormy steps towards Italian unification throughout the 1850s as in her own personal fortunes. Her letters anticipating the tragic death from cancer of her sister Henrietta in November 1860 are as frantic about the treachery of Napoleon III, the supposed saviour of Italy, as over her own grief, and the news of the disastrous Treaty of Villafranca in 1859, when Italy was 'betrayed' to the Austrians by the French, left her totally prostrated. It seemed that her hero Napoleon III had bargained unforgivably with Austria in allowing Franz Joseph to give Lombardy to France, who would cede it to Piedmont in return for a future promise of Nice and Savoy. Napoleon had betrayed all her faith in him as the friend of Italy. Her health from the summer of 1859 was ever more precarious.

The attack that ended in her death in June 1861 had seemed no different from a score of similar ones in what had by then become routine general ill-health, and she mocked Robert gently for his concern. 'Well, you do make an exaggerated case of it!', she declared. Elizabeth herself had no real apprehensions. Unless she had her own private motives, she generally played down her ill-health. But Robert had his own fears now, recognised the disease of her lungs as advanced, and sat at her bedside throughout the night. She died in his arms as 29 June 1861 dawned, still untroubled, her thoughts on their love. She was buried in the Protestant cemetery in Florence on 1 July.

Robert had a last service still to do for her, to collect together her *Last Poems* and see them through the press. Some are of the political situation in Italy ('First News from Villafranca', 'King Victor Emmanuel Entering Florence 1860', 'Garibaldi'), but one that spoke most comfortingly to the shattered husband was 'The Best Thing in the World'. It is a twelve-line poem, a list that moves through the natural world in its consideration ('June rose by May dew impearled', 'Sweet south wind that means no rain', 'Light that never makes you wink'), and lofty abstractions like 'Truth', 'Pleasure', 'Beauty', and 'Memory', and then, having weighed them all, arrives at its conclusion: the best thing in the world is 'Love, when, so, you're loved again'. Elizabeth and Robert had achieved and shared the best thing in the world, and neither forgot it.

It has become another part of the Browning myth that one cause of Elizabeth's death was the death of her hero Cavour. Cavour had become the central focus of her life outside her family. He was the leader of Piedmont, the most powerful of the Italian states, and was at the heart of the movement towards the Unification of Italy. His sudden death in June 1861 (and he was younger than Elizabeth) at the moment when his survival seemed essential if his work was to be completed and national unity preserved, seemed to shatter all her political hopes; she could 'scarcely comprehend the greatness of the vacancy' (L, II, 449).

Ever since childhood she had been inclined to think of politics in terms of individuals, and had always looked up to 'strong men'. From the upstairs room at Hope End she had been affected by the romantic surge of nationalism and liberalism which had swept through Europe in the 1820s, and her earliest hero had been Lord Byron who represented the spirit as it blazed through Southern Europe. His death in Greece in 1824, in the Homeric struggle of the Greeks against their Turkish rulers, became a symbol of the new spirit which the young Elizabeth Barrett had commemorated in one of her first published poems. And she had eagerly read Madame de Stael's monumental study of German nationalism, *De l'Allmagne*, we learn from her notebook, which was one of the influences shaping the politics of Southern and Eastern Europe.

When she grew up Byron was supplanted as a hero by Napoleon III even in the days before the *coup d'état* in 1851, when he was still Louis Napoleon, constitutionally elected President of the Second Republic. In 1852, in spite of the 1848 constitution declaring the republic, he proclaimed himself emperor, and Elizabeth Barrett, though a self-styled Republican, backed him eagerly, glorying in his 'audacity and dexterity'. One of the finest *Poems Before Congress* is a splendid ode, 'Napoleon in Italy', which celebrates his martial valour. Louis Napoleon had grandiose ideas of recreating the days of the First Empire under his famous uncle, and she admired his pursuit of nationalism in the forceful policies of militant diplomacy which were making France an authoritarian and militaristic state. Elizabeth, defending his defiance of the constitution in seizing power, argued that the Assembly which had elected him President was not carrying out the wishes of the people when it denied him a second term, and that there was a higher right than a legal right: 'living people are above the constitution'. She herself was carried away into sympathy by what she called the bravery and promptitude of his last act.

Cavour was her latest hero. It is interesting to see the links which connect the men she most admired. There is a kind of consistency in her apparent *volte face* from the declared republicanism of her idealistic young days at Hope End to her defence of Cavour's sometimes questionable tactics and her open championing of Napoleon's virtual dictatorship. Cavour too openly lost faith in democracy alone, believing that it must in this case be combined with force to expel Austria from northern Italy. Elizabeth admired the 'strong man' in politics, who would dominate society and, if necessary, impose his will by force, and she admired to distraction Cavour's single-handed achievements in Piedmont and his plans for the rest of Italy. It was always, in the end, the individual who was more important than the principle, though she had once declared to Mary Mitford 'I am no Napoleonist. I am simply a democrat' (LM, January 1852). But her views on democracy and the will of the people, however strongly she expressed them at Hope End and elsewhere, show very differently in *Aurora Leigh* and her treatment there of 'the mob'.

Aurora Leigh succeeds in quite other terms than as the manifesto of a failed democrat, of course. Elizabeth Barrett Browning had worked hard at it through the years that led up to the distressing time later in the 1850s, and told her brother George that it was beyond question quite her best work. The winter of 1852-1853 was mild, and both Brownings resolved to make a beginning on major projects, Elizabeth on *Aurora Leigh* and Robert on *Men and Women*. To her concern, Browning had done very little since they came to

Italy in 1846, and his reputation had scarcely recovered after the disaster of *Sordello* in 1840. His mother's death some days after the birth of Pen in 1849 had plunged him into a depression that silenced him for a long period. Then he had been much occupied in learning to paint and in visits to the Uffizi, he spent two hours a day teaching Pen to play the piano, and he organised most of their domestic affairs. He had published volumes of moderate success since *Sordello*, among them *Bells and Pomegranates*, but *Men and Women* was the work he hoped would make his name. His wife as always knew that he was a genius, but on the whole the world did not.

With his wife it was different: she had triumphantly combined marriage with vocation, and *Aurora Leigh* was merely to confirm the popularity of *Poems* (1850) and the volumes since. The narrator of *Aurora Leigh* tells how she arrived at the union of woman and poet: it is the work, the author said, into which her highest convictions upon life and art had entered, and it is the story of Elizabeth Barrett Browning herself.

The book repeated the success of the earlier poems: it appeared in November 1856, and the first edition sold out in a week, the second in a month. Ruskin, a warm friend in London, wrote to Browning and spoke of it as 'the greatest poem in the language, surpassed only by Shakespeare, but not by his sonnets', and moving from hyperbole to hyperbole added in a second letter that it was 'the greatest poem which the century has produced in any language'. Swinburne felt rather the same:

> The advent of *Aurora Leigh* can never be forgotten by any lover of poetry ... Of one thing they may all be sure — they never had read, and never would read, anything in any way comparable with that unique work of audaciously feminine and ambitiously impulsive genius.
>
> ('Aurora Leigh', 6, 3)

George Eliot, writing in the *Westminster Review* in January 1857, spoke of it as 'the greatest poem' by 'a woman of genius', and envied Sara Hennell her sight of Mrs Browning, 'the medium of great and beautiful things' (24 December 1856); and the two women met when George Eliot was in Rome with G.H. Lewes in 1860. Carlyle was gruffly charmed with the poem. He was originally a friend of Browning but now of them both; they dined in Chelsea when they were in England, and once travelled with him to Paris. 'It is difficult to conceive of a more interesting soul ...', she had declared to Anna Jameson (L, II, 21 October 1858). Their friends the Tennysons — they dined with the Laureate in Paris and London, and knew his brother Frederick intimately in Florence — were enthusiastic.

Another very longstanding literary friend with whom the author discussed the poem in detail was Anna Jameson. She was a much published writer of art and literary criticism, with a growing reputation. Elizabeth Barrett had first encountered the work of Mrs Jameson in the upstairs room at Hope End as a girl, where according to her notebook she read the *Diary of an Ennuyée*, a fictional travel account which anticipated Mrs Jameson's more famous travel books, which Elizabeth had also read with enthusiasm. Kenyon had tried to arrange a meeting between them in 1842; when that failed Mrs Jameson had determinedly called in Wimpole Street, and having once broken the barrier of Barrett shyness, had become a regular visitor. Elizabeth described the first visit to Mrs Martin:

> Mrs Jameson, overcoming by kindness, was let in on Saturday last; and sat with me for nearly an hour, and so ran into what my sisters call 'one of my sudden intimacies' that there was an embrace for a farewell!
> (L, 1, 26 November 1844)

Nor was their friendship broken, or even interrupted, by the Brownings' runaway marriage and residence abroad. A great traveller herself, in September 1846 Mrs Jameson had been startled and overjoyed to find a message from Robert Browning at her Paris hotel: 'Come and see your friend and my wife Elizabeth Barrett Browning — Robert Browning'. And she had been a visitor in Florence in the earliest days, alone and with her niece, and stayed regularly at the Casa Guidi. She was, Elizabeth told her sister, 'a high-minded, true, generous woman. Very much I like, yes, and love her' (LS, April 1847). On another occasion they had all been in Paris in 1852, where Elizabeth and Anna Jameson had spent an exciting day together at a military revue. They corresponded freely with each other from different parts of Europe, and met in London; and she was among the most loyal of the Brownings' friends. Her death in 1859 was another of the blows to hit Elizabeth at that time.

One of the topics she discussed with Anna Jameson when *Aurora Leigh* appeared was the similarity between the endings of her poem and *Jane Eyre*, which critics had seized on, but which Elizabeth dismissed impatiently as an inaccurate irrelevance:

> [The] only injury received by Romney in the fire was from a
> blow and from the emotion produced by the circumstances of
> the fire. Not only did he not lose his eyes in the fire, but he
> describes the ruin of the house as no blind man could. He was
> standing there, a spectator ...
> (L, II, 26 December 1856)

Yet the oldest friend to whom Elizabeth wrote to the end went back
beyond Anna Jameson and even Mary Russell Mitford to childhood
days at Hope End. This was Julia Martin. To her Elizabeth described
the work before it was published, in a phrase that became famous,
as 'a novel ... a sort of novel in verse' (L, II, July/August 1855). With
Julia Martin she raised the issue that vexed the critics, the 'coarse-
ness' of *Aurora Leigh*. The poem referred fearlessly to the questions
of prostitution, of rape, of female exploitation, and the poet de-
fended her decision to do so:

> [Y]ou will grant that I don't habitually dabble in the dirt; it's
> not the way of my mind or life. If, therefore, I move certain
> subjects in this work, it is because my conscience was first
> moved in me not to ignore them. What has given most offence
> in the book, more than the story of Marian — far more! — has
> been the reference to the condition of women in our cities,
> which a woman oughtn't to refer to, by any manner of means,
> says the conventional tradition. If a woman ignores these
> wrongs, then may woman as a sex continue to suffer them;
> there is no help for any of us — let us be dumb and die.
> (L, II, February 1857)

She discussed with her correspondent the moral responsibilities of
the artist and the response of her readers (*The Athenaeum* said, 'To
some [*Aurora Leigh*] will be so much rank foolishness — to others
almost a spiritual revelation'), a question she and Mrs Martin had
already debated when Mrs Gaskell's *Ruth* was published in 1853,
and had scandalised the public in much the same way.

Mrs Martin is the correspondent through whom we have the most
complete perspective of Elizabeth as both Barrett and Browning at
all stages of her life. Elizabeth writes to her regularly and frequently
from first Devon and London and then Paris and Italy; but long
before that Mrs Martin makes frequent appearances in her early

diary as a regular visitor to Hope End, a hostess in Colwall and a companion on excursions in the surrounding countryside, among all the details of middle-class social life in Herefordshire. After one afternoon spent with the Martins in Colwall 'to play cricket and drink tea', Elizabeth remarked with some of the pertness of youth on the oddness that 'Mrs Martin, who, I think likes me, and I, who, I am sure, like Mrs Martin, should be oil and water together' (*Diary*, 74). But Elizabeth had always been happier expressing herself on paper than face to face. Letters were always the most congenial medium for her to conduct a relationship. In them she was relaxed, animated, warm and witty. She began a correspondence with Mrs Martin from the moment they left Hope End for Sidmouth in 1832 which lasted until her death, and during the time the Barretts were in Devon Mrs Martin is invited to join the initiates who know Elizabeth as 'Ba'.

All the high points of her life are recorded at length and in detail in the correspondence with her friend at Colwall. Browning's name appears from the occasion of his first letter, initially as 'the poet ... the king of the mystics', then in warmer terms as their friendship grew until, less than a month after their wedding, she is writing a long account from Pisa, their first home, of how her life has changed. It is the longest, fullest extant version of what happened that day, and the weeks that followed; and Pen's birth and babyhood are recorded in similar detail. The last letter, written only a short time before her death, acknowledges photographs sent from Herefordshire and a book sent by Mrs Martin as a present for Pen.

Mrs Martin was the means by which Elizabeth always stayed in contact with Ledbury. Elizabeth never lost touch with her roots. Mrs Martin's letters covered the lives and times of the people among whom Elizabeth had grown up — the Martins, the Biddulphs, the Commelines, the Cockses, all neighbouring families in Eastnor, Malvern, Matton, and the Bartons. Elizabeth's letters give a picture of herself as she evolves from the shy, diffident young woman whose most significant experience is contained in the view to Great Malvern from the Wyche, to the assured wife, mother and artist, whose maturest work ranks (according to some) with Shakespeare's, and whose territory is Europe.

Her correspondent in Herefordshire, in fact, is an invaluable catalyst. Her view of the situation at Hope End and later Wimpole Street, from a position untrammelled by family loyalties, was able to be dispassionate. She could silently in Colwall will Elizabeth to stand up to her father, and could applaud without hesitation when she did. She wrote at once, for example, expressing the warmest support for Elizabeth's marriage to Browning (and later Henrietta's to Surtees Cook), and she wrote afterwards to Edward Barrett begging him to forgive his daughters.

She wrote more than once suggesting that Elizabeth should revisit Herefordshire, where she had spent half her life, and inviting them both to Colwall. In earlier years Elizabeth had written wistfully for details of Hope End. But now her associations with Hope End and Ledbury concerned too much of Bro, and were too poignant for her even to consider such a thing. She explained regretfully,

> There is only one event in my life which never loses its bitterness ... which was and is my grief — I never had but one brother who loved and comprehended me ... I never could bear it. The past would be too strong for me. Torquay [where Bro drowned] has made the neighbourhood at Hope End impossible for me ...
> (L, II, July/August 1855)

Although she had written to R.H. Horne of the Malvern hills, the hills of Piers Plowman's vision, which seemed, she said, 'my native hills. Beautiful, beautiful hills they are!' (L, I, 5 November 1843), she could not return to the enchanted land. She wrote to her sister that though she loved the Martins ('they are true friends whom I love'), Herefordshire, with all its associations of Bro, 'is all bitter with the bitterness of my heart. I could not sit and eat and sleep in it, I feel still' (LS, 7 July 1850). They met instead in Paris in 1852, with joy on both sides, and on a variety of other occasions, but always on neutral ground.

Life changed twice for Elizabeth, once when Hope End was sold and the Barretts moved — after an interval — to London, and once when Robert Browning (in Miss Mitford's words) carried her off her feet to a new world in Italy. There was no going back from either of the changes, and she would not have wished to go back. The happiness of her life in Italy, as wife, as mother, as artist supreme among women, was something in which she found it difficult to believe. Her unlooked-for marriage late in life, completed with the unexpected joy of motherhood was, she told Mrs Martin, 'the happiness and honour of my life' (L, II, August 1851). Next to it, she added, 'Hope End ... is nothing. I have been happier in my own home since, than I was there and then'.

But in earlier letters to her friend she had written in quite different terms. Until her life changed for the second time, and offered happiness and honour in Florence, Hope End was home. Once she had written in anguished tones

> ... the thought stands before me sometimes like an object in a dream, that I shall see no more those hills and trees which seemed to me once almost like portions of my existence.
> (L, I, 19 December 1834)

And another time, musing on home she declared, 'I may *like* other places — but no other place can appear to me to deserve that name' (L, I, 27 September 1832).

Bibliography

Unpublished Sources

Notebook of Elizabeth Barrett 1822-1824, Margaret Clapp Library (Special Collections), Wellesley College, Massachusetts

Primary Sources

Diary by EBB: The Unpublished Diary of Elizabeth Barrett Browning 1831-1832, edited by Philip Kelley and Ronald Hudson (Athens, Ohio: Ohio University Press, 1969)

Autobiographical Essays by Elizabeth Barrett Browning (in *The Brownings' Correspondence*, Vol I), edited by Philip Kelly and Ronald Hudson (Wedgestone Press, 1984)

The Brownings' Correspondence, Vol I, edited by Philip Kelly and Ronald Hudson (Wedgestone Press, 1984)

Elizabeth Barrett Browning's Letters to Mrs David Ogilvy, edited by Peter N. Heydon and Philip Kelley (New York: New York Times Book Co., Quadrangle and Browning Institute, 1973)

The Letters of Elizabeth Barrett Browning, edited by Frederick L. Kenyon, 2 vols (London: Macmillan, 1897)

Elizabeth Barrett to Miss Mitford: The Unpublished Letters of Elizabeth Barrett Browning to Mary Russell Mitford, edited by Betty Miller (London: John Murray, 1954)

Letters of the Brownings to George Barrett, edited by Paul Landis with Ronald E. Freeman (Urbana: University of Illinois Press, 1958)

Elizabeth Barrett Browning: Letters to her Sister, 1846-1859 (London: John Murray, 1929)

Elizabeth Barrett to Mr Boyd: Unpublished Letters of Elizabeth Barrett Browning to Hugh Stuart Boyd, edited by Barbara P. McCarthy (London: John Murray, 1955)

Letters of Elizabeth Barrett Browning Addressed to Richard Hengist Horne, 2 vols, edited by S.R.Townshend Mayer, 2 vols, London: Richard Bentley and Son, 1877

The Religious Opinions of Elizabeth Barrett Browning, as Expressed in Three Letters Adressed to William Merry, Esq, J.P., London: Hodder and Stoughton, 1906.

Secondary Sources

Ellen Moers, *Literary Women* (Garden City: Doubleday, 1976)

Angela Deighton, *Elizabeth Barrett Browning* (Brighton: Harvester, 1986)

Margaret Forster, *Elizabeth Barrett Browning: The Life and Loves of a Poet* (New York: St. Martin's Press, 1988)

Helen Cooper, *Elizabeth Barrett Browning, Woman and Artist* (Chapel Hill and London: University of North Carolina Press, 1988)

Dorothy Mermin, *Elizabeth Barrett Browning: The Origins of a New Poetry* (Chicago: University of Chicago Press, 1989)

Peter Dally, *Elizabeth Barrett Browning: A Psychological Portrait* (London: Macmillan, 1989)

Acknowledgements

I gratefully acknowledge the assistance, kindness, patience and encouragement of a large number of people throughout the time I have been engaged with this book. Their help, in every form, has made the task so pleasant. I am grateful in particular to the Margaret Clapp Library (Special Collections), Wellesley College, Massachusetts; Edward Moulton Barrett; Lilian Sanders (Parish Archivist, Ledbury); Colin and Ann Beevers; William Price; Helen Dumbleton; and Beryl Doyle.

Barbara Dennis

Acknowledgements are due to the Provost and Fellows of Eton College for permission to reproduce illustrations 1, 3, 4, 5, 6 and 7. Acknowledgements for other illustrations are due to the Fitzwilliam Museum, Cambridge (9), Hereford and Worcester County Council (2), Margaret Clapp Library, Wellesley College, Massachusetts (8), and the National Portrait Gallery (10).

The cover illustration is by permission of Capt. Gordon Moulton Barrett.

The publisher would like to thank Michael Meredith of Eton College Library and Philip Kelley for their assistance in locating illustrations.

Series Afterword

The Border country is that region between England and Wales which is upland and lowland, both and neither. Centuries ago kings and barons fought over these Marches without their national allegiance ever being settled. In our own time, referring to his childhood, that eminent borderman Raymond Williams once said 'We talked of "The English" who were not us, and "The Welsh" who were not us'. It is beautiful, gentle, intriguing and often surprising. It displays majestic landscapes, which show a lot, and hide some more. People now walk it, poke into its cathedrals and bookshops, and fly over or hang-glide from its mountains, yet its mystery remains.

In cultural terms the region is as fertile as (in parts) its agriculture and soil. The continued success of the Three Choirs Festival and the growth of the border town of Hay as a centre of the second-hand book trade have both attracted international recognition. The present series of introductory books is offered in the light of such events. Writers as diverse as Mary Webb, Raymond Williams and Wilfred Owen are seen in the special light — perhaps that cloudy golden twilight so characteristic of the region — of their origin in this area or association with it. There are titles too, though fewer, on musicians and painters. The Gloucestershire composers such as Samuel Sebastian Wesley, and painters like David Jones, bear an imprint of border woods, rivers, villages and hills.

How wide is the border? Two, five or fifteen miles each side of the boundary; it depends on your perspective, on the placing of the nearest towns, on the terrain itself, and on history. In the time of Offa and after, Hereford itself was a frontier town, and Welsh was spoken there even in the nineteenth century. True border folk traditionally did not recognise those from even a few miles away. Today, with greater mobility, the crossing of boundaries is easier, whether for education, marriage, art or leisure. For myself, who spent some childhood years in Herefordshire and a decade of middle age cross-ing between England and Wales once a week, I can only say that as you approach the border you feel it. Suddenly you are in that finally elusive terrain, looking from a bare height down onto the plain, or from lower land up to a gap in the hills, and you want to explore it, maybe not to return.

This elusiveness pertains to the writers and artists too. It is often difficult to decide who is border, to what extent and with what impact on their work. The urbane Elizabeth Barrett Browning, prominent figure of the salons of London and Italy in her time, spent virtually all her life until her late twenties outside Ledbury in Herefordshire, and this fact is being seen by current critics and scholars as of more and more significance. The twentieth century 'English pastoral' composers — with names like Parry, Howells and Vaughan Williams — were nearly all border people. One wonders whether border country is now suddenly found on the English side of the Severn Bridge, and how far even John Milton's *Comus*, famous for its first production in Ludlow Castle, is in any sense such a work. Then there is the fascinating Uxbridge-born Peggy Eileen Whistler, transposed in the 1930s into Margiad Evans to write her (epilepsis-based) visionary novels set near her adored Ross-on-Wye and which today still retain a magical charm. Further north: could Barbara Pym, born and raised in Oswestry, even remotely be called a border writer? Most people would say that the poet A.E. Housman was far more so, yet he hardly visited the county after which his chief book of poems, *A Shropshire Lad*, is named. Further north still: there is the village of Chirk on the boundary itself, where R.S. Thomas had his first curacy; there is Gladstone's Hawarden Library, just outside Chester and actually into Clwyd in Wales itself; there is intriguingly the Wirral town of Birkenhead, where Wilfred Owen spent his adolescence and where his fellow war poet Hedd Wyn was awarded his Chair — posthumously.

On the Welsh side the names are different. The mystic Ann Griffiths; the metaphysical poet Henry Vaughan; the astonishing nineteenth century symbolist novelist Arthur Machen (in Linda Dowling's phrase, 'Pater's prose as registered by Wilde'); and the remarkable Thomas Olivers of Gregynog, associated with the writing of the well-known hymn 'Lo He comes with clouds descending'. Those descending clouds ...; in border country the scene hangs overhead, and it is easy to indulge in unwarranted speculation. Most significant perhaps is the difference between the two peoples on either side. From England, the border meant the enticement of emptiness, a strange unpopulated land, going up and up into the hills. From Wales, the border meant the road to London, to the university, or to employment, whether by droving sheep, or later to the industries of Birmingham and Liverpool. It also meant the enemy, since borders and boundaries are necessarily political. Much is shared, yet different languages are spoken, in more than one sense.

With certain notable exceptions, the books in this series are short introductory studies of one person's work or some aspect of it. There are normally no indexes. The bibliography lists main sources referred to in the text and sometimes others, for those who would like to pursue the topic further. The authors reflect the diversity of their subjects. They are specialists or academics; critics or biographers; poets or musicians themselves; or ordinary people with, however, an established reputation of writing imaginatively and directly about what moves them. They are of various ages, both sexes, Welsh and English, border people themselves or from further afield.

To those who explore the matter, the subjects — the writers, painters and composers written about — seem increasingly united by a particular kind of vision. This holds good however diverse they are in other, main ways; and of course they are diverse indeed. One might scarcely associate, it would seem, Raymond Williams with Samuel Sebastian Wesley, or Dennis Potter with Thomas Traherne. But one has to be careful in such assumptions. The epigraph to Bruce Chatwin's twentieth century novel *On the Black Hill* is a passage from the seventeenth century mystic writer Jeremy Taylor. Thomas Traherne himself is the subject of a recent American study which puts Traherne's writings into dialogue with European philosopher-critics like Martin Heidegger, Jacques Derrida and Jacques Lacan. And a current best-selling writer of thrillers, Ellis Peters, sets her stories in a Shrewsbury of the late medieval Church with a cunning quiet monk as her ever-engaging sleuth.

The vision (name incidentally of the farmhouse in Chatwin's novel) is something to do with the curious border light already mentioned. To avoid getting sentimental and mystic here — though border writers have sometimes been both — one might suggest that this effect is meteorological. Perhaps the sun's rays are refracted through skeins of dew and mist that hit the stark mountains and low hills at curious ascertainable angles, with prismatic results. Not that rainbows are the point in our area: it is more the contrasts of gold, green and grey. Some writers never mention it. They don't have to. But all the artists of the region see it, are affected by it, and transpose their highly different emanations of reality through its transparencies. Meanwhile, on the ground, the tourist attractions draw squads from diverse cultural and ethnic origins; agriculture enters the genetic-engineering age; New Age travellers are welcome and unwelcome; and the motorway runs up parallel past all — 'Lord of the M5', as the poet Geoffrey Hill has dubbed the Saxon king Offa, he of the dyke which bisects the region where it can still be identified. The region has its uniqueness, then, and a statistically above-average number of writers and artists (we have identified over fifty clear candidates so far) have drawn something from it, which it is the business of the present series to elucidate.

Despite the efforts of Margaret Forster and others to rectify the matter, it is still only just dawning on many people that Elizabeth Barrett Browning, of London and Italy fame, spent twenty-six successive years of her childhood and early life in the countryside near Ledbury in Herefordshire. Hardly most people's idea of a 'border' writer or person, she is for that reason something of a test case, if early experience has as profound an effect on our lives as is usually agreed. The plain fact is that Elizabeth never forgot the place and never ceased to love it. That Elizabeth's home, Hope End, still has this powerful effect is made beautifully clear in this book's introduction by Patrica Hegarty, with her husband the present owners and residents. Barbara Dennis's account of the effect of the Hope End years on Elizabeth's life, both at the time and after, uses much new diary and notebook material from those years and has not previously been told in this way. As such it adds substantially to our understanding of not only Elizabeth Barrett Browning herself but of border experience and its expression in literature more widely.

John Powell Ward

The Author

Barbara Dennis is Head of Victorian Studies and Senior Lecturer in English at the University of Wales in Lampeter. She has previously published a study of Charlotte Young, *Charlotte Younge, Novelist of the Oxford Movement* (Mellen, 1992) and is a co-editor of *Reform and Intellectual Debate in Victorian England* (Routledge, 1987). She has also edited an edition of Trollope's *The Warden* for Everyman paperbacks (1993) and Younge's *The Daisy Chain* for Virago (1988). Her edition of Younge's *The Heir of Ratcliffe* is forthcoming from Oxford University Press.